Getting a Life

America's Challenge to Grow Up

Getting a Life
© 1996 by Leslie Dreyfous
All rights reserved.
Printed in the United States

No portion of this book may be reproduced in any form without written from the publisher, Gold Leaf Press, 2533 North Carson St., Suite 1544, Carson City, NV 89706

Library of Congress Cataloging-in-Publication Data

Dreyfous, Leslie
Getting a life : America's challenge to grow up / Leslie Dreyfous.
    p.   cm.
ISBN 1-882723-13-9
1. United States—Social conditions—1980- 2. Social change—United States 3. Community organization—United States. 4. Community power—United States. I. Title.
HN59.2.D74 1996
306'.0973—dc20   96-12053
                                              CIP

10 9 8 7 6 5 4 3 2 1

Getting a Life

America's Challenge to Grow Up

Leslie Dreyfous

GOLD LEAF PRESS

For William Bell Jr. and Jack,
two grown-ups.

Contents

Chapter One
Getting a Clue: Who Ever Said Growing Up Would Be Easy?   1

Chapter Two
Getting Real: Facing the Fact That You Can't Have It All   26

Chapter Three
Getting a Grip: Facing the Demons   53

Chapter Four
Getting Over It: Moving Forward Means Defying Despair   73

Chapter Five
Getting in the Act: True Grown-ups Aren't Afraid to Play   99

Chapter Six
Getting Together: Maturity Is about Daring to Make Change   129

Chapter Seven
Getting a Life: Don't You Know It's Wherever You Are?   159

Acknowledgments

This book has been loaned to me, culled from the lives of so many strangers I've come to call friends. In taking a risk, you gave me a break. In opening your hearts, often under difficult circumstances, you pointed the way home. Without your voices—those that show up in these pages and those that do not—I could never have reported a single story. I would never have gone on what has been a remarkable journey. You gave my work life and gave my world light. I can only thank you, then thank you once again, for that.

I'd also like to send a bouquet to my long-suffering colleagues at The Associated Press, most especially my editors, Kristin Gazlay and Jerry Schwartz, without whose sharp eyes and senses of humor the work on which this book is based might never have found its way to the wire. You didn't "make me up," but you did provide me a place to grow.

To Curtis Taylor, Stan Zenk and Paul Rawlins at Gold Leaf Press: You've been a writer's fondest dream by being editors who speak frankly, listen well and, most of all, care. I am likewise indebted to Bill Kovach, the staff and my fellow fellows at Harvard's Nieman Foundation. You all gave me the year that it took. In particular to Lorie Hearn. In your keen blue eyes I found more than a perpetually astute critic, more than the best of friends. In those eyes I have found "something like" the point of it all. To "the group"—Ellen Fitzpatrick, Kathy Hirsch, Melissa Ludtke, Sara Rimer and Liz Weld Nolan—all I can say is that without your smarts and suppers I would never truly have started.

Finally, to my far-flung family and friends, you did all the rest. You kept me afloat with so much laughter, patience and love. You've given me the foundation, the bricks, the mortar and steel. Most of all, you've given me great heart. Thank you all for the many gifts.

—NEW YORK CITY, SPRING 1996

A Brief Introduction

Sometimes when I'm out on the road, a reporter speeding along toward whatever random story, the miles suddenly close in and the silence bears down. This is when, if only to hear the sound of a voice, I ask myself that age-old road-trip question: "When are we going to get there?"

Sometimes this gives me a laugh. Sometimes there are tears in my eyes.

There is no parent around to humor or hush me up, and anyway I am hardly a child. Only one person is in the car, and she's sitting behind the wheel. The route, the speed, the style, the spirit of the drive, they are all up to me.

How clammy it feels to be adrift a million miles from home. Worse still is the feeling that, no matter how many miles you cover, the trip is never quite done. You still haven't arrived at that ideal place where finally you are comfortable and safe. So you drive on and drive on some more, drift further and further, while all the time that home of your dreams keeps on slipping away.

I'd covered a great distance before truly beginning to grasp that, wherever you are, you're already there.

This book is about growing up, getting a grip, giving a damn. And it's about the many people, in most cases strangers, who helped me finally to understand that there is no happy hearth waiting over some next hill. Home does not come in a bolt from heaven, nor is it some new gimmick on sale down at the mall. It's the way we live in the world every day, the plot of land that, side-by-side with others, we painstakingly tend. I'd driven thousands of miles and written hundreds of newspaper stories before I fully began to embrace this, before the voices started coming together and the light flickered on in my head.

An old friend, a reporter whose judgment I respect, once told me that I had a tendency to see barbecues and basketball hoops in everyone's backyard. He cautioned against finding American dreams where they did not exist. I took his observation seriously and ever since have been self-conscious, ready to rein myself in, which is not a bad thing. And yet, I've continued to see them. The basketball hoops have cropped up more often than not. I've also seen tremendous treachery and sadness, all manner of loss. But more than treachery and sadness, at the heart of the most difficult stories and abject disappointment, I've mostly found something like hope.

Out there are millions of people who understand the meaning of community, yearn for it and, in ways large and small, build toward it every day. Don't let anyone tell you that Americans are not interested in the issues or have no thoughts but for themselves. Don't let anyone tell you that there is no vision, that there are no visionaries. I've met heroism, over and over again, in all kinds of faces. Drive into any town, walk down any city block, and you'll find these citizens quietly holding their families and neighborhoods together. They are not alone, though too often they feel that way. Between the benumbing news headlines and stress of complex daily life, many of us feel squeezed on all sides. There doesn't seem to be any time or opportunity to explore, no room to speak, no place to be heard. Some of us hang in, fight on, despite feeling overwhelmed. Many of us look away, lazily tune out.

Some of us act like grown-ups. Many of us behave like overgrown children.

It is often said that we leave this world just as we come to it: Alone. But what we do in between, the lives we touch and the ways in which we care, ultimately defines who we are. There is nothing simple about moving into the fray. Making an investment with your heart, accepting responsibility for what lies ahead, requires commitment and fearlessness and, very often, sacrifice. But then, only fools think life isn't about hard work.

Most of us learn at a fairly young age that good deeds aren't necessarily rewarded, that much in life is anything but fair, that strangers can hurt us and people we love sometimes disappoint. In the end, though, it is the degree to which we face down and drive through the rough spots that describes who we are and the legacy we leave for generations to come.

True grown-ups don't just show up. They stay. No matter how uncertain the future or delayed the reward. They are the ones who link arms with each other—even when it is hard, even when great differences in ethnicity, class, sex, geography, age, politics, lifestyle come in between. True grown-ups waste no time building bunkers against weakness and frustration. They accept these things, even find humor in their inevitability, then determinedly trundle on. They embody the faith of small children and the dignity found in the oldest, most battered of human hearts.

True grown-ups do more than live in homes. They build them—not tomorrow, but today.

The turning point

in the process of growing up

is when you discover

the core of strength within you

that survives all the hurt.

Max Lerner,
"The Unfinished Country"

Getting a Clue

Who Ever Said Growing Up Would Be Easy?

In the locker room at work the other day I overheard two women—mothers with laundry and shopping to do, kids to pick up, bills to pay, no money to spare and a long subway ride out to Queens ahead—swapping complaints when one stopped midsentence, paused, then said: "It's like the party's over, girl. We got work to do. And it ain't gonna stop."

To which her friend replied: "You got that right. If they'd told me you were gonna have all this responsibility, I wouldn't have grown up. I would have stayed little all my life."

I smiled. That about summed up how we all feel, at least from time to time.

As I've traveled the country as a national writer reporting for The Associated Press, several themes have played again and again like a fugue, shared and built upon by people of all ages, classes, races; people with very different backgrounds, tastes and political bents. So many of us have felt somehow displaced. This isn't how it was supposed to be. We were going to have it all. Instead, many

2 Getting a Clue

Americans simply feel overloaded. Even cheated. Few have not felt brokenhearted about how violent and crazed and lonely the world seems to have become.

We wonder: Has so much been shattered that nothing can be fixed?

It is not easy to see the way. Reports come live from bloody shooting scenes or in soundbites coined by politicians that no one trusts. They come via satellite from Bosnia, Rwanda, Haiti. In Oklahoma City, homegrown terrorism appeared at our door. People tell me constantly that they feel bombarded by more information than they can digest. Studies tell them that the nuclear family is terminally fractured and morality all but lost among the young. Citizens find sadness on the streets they walk and frustration in perpetually paying taxes that never seem to clean their cities up. Everywhere there are stark facts and frightening predictions.

But despite the litany of woes, America is still fat and rich. In fact, we're so blessed that we have the time and opportunity to whine, a luxury unknown to a huge portion of the world, to the many struggling for basic freedoms or food to eat. I have watched people who complain they are drowning in debt waste hours in mega-malls jammed with merchandise they don't really need. I've listened to dieters obsess on their weight while inhaling fat-laden cheeseburgers and double-orders of fries. Men and women have lectured me about the sorry lack of a work ethic today while balanced at noontime on stools in riverboat casinos and honkytonk bars. I've heard teenage dropouts blame their bankrupt dreams on adults because, hey, they're the ones who screwed everything up. Citizens have denounced epidemic poverty, crime and aimlessness among the young time and again, only sheepishly to admit that they've not yet quite found time to volunteer. I've written whole stories about mothers and fathers who are too busy to be with their friends, their neighbors, their kids. But somehow millions tune in each evening for hour on hour of mindless prime-time TV. Taxpayers have told me repeatedly that they want better roads, better public schools, better health care. But government? They don't even bother to vote. In plain terms, though certainly not across the board, we have been terribly spoiled.

I've thought a lot in recent months about a word I heard fairly frequently while growing up: Gumption. The frankly sappy film *Forrest Gump*, which confounded Hollywood types by doing astonishingly well against big-action thrillers, has given the term its own spin. But around our house years ago, gumption had vaguely to do with getting up off your rear end and committing to life. It had to do not just with getting by, but actually aspiring to contribute; with doing more than the minimum, more than just enough.

There was never any particular rationale for having gumption. It wasn't recommended as a way to make money or gain recognition. It wasn't offered as a means to any ends. The payoff was in having done the right thing, in having done all you could do. Movie critics and social commentators, some cynical and some not, have examined the *Forrest Gump* phenomenon fairly closely. It has been suggested that the movie naively recommended being dumb and nice as a surefire way to wealth and fame. But it seems to me that this formulation entirely misses the point and may miss what it is that drew so many people to the film. The fictional title character wasn't just a dope whose terminal kindness paid off big. He was a guy who, simple or not, did the right things. He confronted a variety of situations with a basic, innate dignity that had nothing to do with politics or puffery, everything to do with unwaveringly acting on a fundamental instinct for decency and fair play.

The urge to withdraw is understandable when the future looks frightening and the people who share our concerns, whether close by or not, somehow seem too far away. It is often all we can do to look out for ourselves because, well, who else will? Gumption, though, is about doing the right things even when it's unclear that anyone else will join in, even when we are fed up or scared. It's about understanding that there is no payoff, except the finest one of all: a sense of purpose and pride.

I heard about gumption a lot as a sullen teenager. It was among a host of words my mother and a long string of nuns used to preach, words like *citizenship* and *sacrifice* and *self-respect*. They weren't easy concepts and they didn't make being a teenager any easier, but they did provide for a soul in adulthood. Without such anchors, it's easy to lose your bearings, forget that we are all bound together in this tenuous enterprise called life. Adolescence is about feeling suddenly alone in a bewildering world that is anything but safe. Adulthood is about making a life.

It often seems to me, though, that instead of growing up we've gotten stuck in what amounts to a sort of national adolescence. We wonder: How am *I* doing? How am *I* affected? Self-absorption is a hallmark of the growing-up years. It adds to an already unnerving time a hobbling sense of isolation. Who am I anyway, and what can I call mine? Like most teenagers, Americans are fundamentally good people. We're just adjusting to a new world, learning slowly that not all things can be seen strictly in terms of ourselves, that sometimes life is best seen in terms of one another. You can slam the bedroom door and blare music, experiment with drugs, fantasize about a future in which you're perennially successful and self-possessed, rage at everyone and find everyone else to blame. But you are still alone, and you still know that right outside lies the roiling mess that sent you running for shelter. Deep down you know it's a mess that won't magically go away.

In life, you have to go through to get through, they say. The most fortunate children start out bolstered and protected and free. There is no responsibility, no limitation, no reason to believe that any need can't be met, any hunger easily sated. In hitting adolescence, the kaleidoscope suddenly shifts. The lens now may be murky, the view anything but nice. There are new feelings, those of insecurity and those of loneliness. And often, at least for awhile, there is the powerful urge to retreat. As a nation, perhaps this is in part what we have done.

America's post–World War II years provided something like an idyllic childhood, full of expansion and expectation unknown to generations that had come before. Not everyone prospered, but more did than at any other time in history. Perhaps blinded by the remarkable bounty and promise of limitless opportunity, puberty has come as a particular shock. The veils have fallen away one after the other before troubling realities. We've got a welfare system that does not work, an economy wrenched by restructuring and old institutions that now seem half undone.

We thought growing up was mostly about finding ourselves, but we found out instead how easily the sense of family and community could be lost. We believed in self-fulfillment, in our right to personal liberty, but perhaps forgot that neither holds much meaning when shadowed by violence and despair. We have migrated from coast to coast, abandoned familiar rituals, moved reflexively forward only to look back nostalgically. We've devoted more than a decade to "me," to preserving what's "mine." It's been several decades now, a long period extending through the 1970s and '80s and into the '90s, during which we've tended to ourselves—sometimes to the exclusion of all else. "If I only had (fill in the blank), then I'd be happy. Just think of what great things I could do!" Somehow, though, the pot of gold has only grown more elusive, brilliant rainbows ever harder to find. For many, as time has marched along, the colors have gone nearly flat.

Many Americans have sought safety and quick comfort by withdrawing behind closed doors. But even the most stubborn of adolescents eventually figures out that there is no true gain, no real protection, in hiding from the big bad world. Eventually most teenagers decide to venture out.

Those who do not, those who obstinately remain disengaged, are forever lost behind slammed doors.

• • •

I've made my life as a reporter for many reasons. I might tell you that it is a drive for justice, a hunger to tell stories that need to be told. I might tell you that it's a creative thing, a love of words and their music, the urge to make some small order of daily chaos. I might tell you that it's about adventure, the chance to explore foreign places and people, to make a living of learning. And all of these things would be true. But flowing beneath them there has always been something else. It is the underbelly, the less noble side of my chosen profession. I make my living as a sort of social voyeur, comfortable being at the scene but not in it; at ease wrestling with chunks of unwieldy emotion, so long as the emotions in question are not my own.

I've liked hanging two steps back, far enough away to limit vulnerability but close enough, always close enough, to see. From this vantage point it has been possible to make complex things simple, spin overwhelming gray areas into reasonably tidy swatches of black and white. Under the pressure of deadlines and the limitations imposed by narrow newspaper columns, sometimes under overwhelmingly sad circumstances, reporters construct as best we can a story that is not so large or confusing that it's altogether indigestible. It is human nature to prefer things wrapped up in neat little packages, even when it's a stretch, a conceit. It's no coincidence that these neat little packages have sometimes gotten in the way of my heart.

When not out helping to cover an earthquake, flood or some other breaking news story, most of the long-term feature projects I've reported for The Associated Press have been based out of a mobile office, namely a subcompact rental car launched from any number of anonymous airports. Often my starting points have been determined by something as serendipitous as wanting to plunk down in a state I'd never visited before or as practical as the great price a travel agent was able to get on a ticket to this city or that. Sometimes I think, had my New York editors known exactly how randomly these excursions were designed, they might not have been so willing to let me wander off as I did. Mostly, though, I think they knew exactly the score and let me go anyway. They gave me the reporter's most treasured gift: rambling time.

They gave me time that might be described as wasted: long lunches in diners whose menus hadn't changed in years, lazy hours with young mothers in a public park, small-town merchants taking stock, urban students with goals yet to form and suburban commuters late for their trains. I had time to sit in people's kitchens, listen to Sunday sermons, share a beer at an out-of-the way bar. While out pursuing stories on our political and social pulse, I also had the space to travel—not just in my rental car, but in my mind. Roving aimlessly will do that to you.

8 Getting a Clue

It is a luxury that opens the heart and all kinds of doors.

Because I had no immediate deadline stories to file and no place to be, I could do on these trips what I find nearly impossible to do in "real life." I could abandon control, let things be messy. No one I met had to be a stereotype or provide a balancing quote for tomorrow's paper. Time on the road would take on a rhythm entirely different from the one that modulated my time in New York. There was no newspaper at the door when I awoke in the morning, no subway to catch or meeting to attend, no leaky faucet to fix or frayed relationship to mend. Jokingly, I've often told friends that on these trips life was reduced to a sort of hunt-and-forage mentality. The goal was to talk to as many people as possible and still find someplace to sleep and something to eat before the day's end.

When I consider this mentality from a distance, it seems very strange. So extremely disconnected.

And yet, on these trips I was always fully alive. I remember the interior of every hotel room, the ones I cried in and the ones that had a remote control for the TV. I developed an affinity for the quirky places that were family owned and a reflexive sense of relief when the sign for certain chains finally cropped up along a darkened highway that threatened to stretch into infinity. I recall all the meals: the sublime fried catfish lunch served up behind a gas station in Arkansas, the quiet moment after dinner was blessed in a soup kitchen in Detroit, the nights when I had neither energy nor appetite enough to pursue eating at all. Sometimes I felt the strangeness, felt disoriented by being a little bit everywhere and nowhere at all. Rarely, though, did I ever truly want to go home. Perhaps because, like so many people, I wasn't quite sure where home might be.

When I was growing up in northern California during the 1960s and '70s, home seemed to be a relative thing. So much was changing so quickly, half of our parents caught up in trying to replicate "Ozzie and Harriet," the other half divorced, separated or enrolled in some kind of self-actualization program through which, after having "found" themselves, they might have decided to divorce or separate. Regardless of whether your parents were hippies or community-pillar types, there was a certain surface quality and impermanency to life. And it was incongruent. Around me—all across the United States as well as in my own hometown—there was so much privilege and opportunity. And at the same time, there were so many adults and near-adults flailing about in search of something more. For a convent schoolgirl now a teenager at the big public high, it was all a little schizophrenic. I'd grown up with the religious ideals of self-sacrifice and discipline only to come of age in a world where earnestness was decidedly unhip. I'd been born to a rock-solid family, one we kids thought was tightly knit, only to discover as time moved on that marriage wasn't necessarily forever, that loved ones sometimes slip far out of reach. Despite being profoundly connected to ritual rhythms, familiar coastal landscapes, the colors and scents of my childhood, for whatever reasons I started plotting my escape at about the age of ten. A few years later, I was gone. A long time passed before I looked back.

It's hard to know what creates a psychic limp, the things that send us staggering into adulthood without any sure sense of balance. But when you strip away all the window dressing and voguish excuses, when you get down to the feeble truth, there is usually a squalling baby hidden somewhere inside. I'm not talking here about a pop-psych "wounded child within." I'm talking about plain old human orneriness, garden-variety crankiness, nameless agitation in the form of hungers we can't seem to fulfill.

Getting a Clue

Sometimes it's as if without thinking twice we scrambled up to a very high place, then made the mistake of looking down. Everything is blurry and far away. Nothing feels quite real. Above all, out on the precipice, we are very small and vulnerable. Sometimes angry, sometimes sad.

Around the time life started confusing me in a big way, a high priest of the self-help movement known as EST visited my high school social studies class (like I said, this was California in the '70s). I resisted the guy right away. But despite this, one image he conjured has stuck in my head ever since: the image of a world in which millions of people are tearing about, frantically looking for love and acceptance, so completely preoccupied with themselves that no one has anything left to give. Everyone with hands outstretched, clutching and hungry. No arms extended, ready with an embrace.

Somewhere between the outer poles of give and take, between paralysis and instant flight, between reflexive self-interest and useless martyrdom, there is a saner common ground. The mark of maturity is finding that balance, integrating your personal, selfish needs with communal obligations that go far beyond. Every time I cover a disaster of some type, I marvel at how we Americans rally and roll up our sleeves when the chips are down. Give us a crisis—something to sandbag or a holiday drive to support or a funeral to attend—and immediately, generously we respond. But then, like adolescents exhausted by our own dramatic outbursts, soon enough we retreat into the safety of our own little worlds. Back and forth we go, in perpetual fits of national moodswing.

I've been guilty of much the same. Give me an extreme, something to rebel against, and I'm there. Ask me to stay, to wade through the tough parts and well, what's the point? I'm moving on. This has been one of the best parts of being a reporter. Drop in, bleed awhile, all the time knowing you're soon moving on. Some years passed before the emptiness got me, before I began to slip through that hole in the middle.

Maybe growing up begins when we realize truly how much there is to lose and how fine a thing having something to lose can be. Maybe like the lyric from a Janis Joplin song I scrawled in my teen-age diary said: "Freedom's just another word for nothing left to lose." The words meant something to me because I was falling in love for the first time and hated it so. My heart was out there and it seemed certain that he would soon move on. And so he did, and so I got better as time went along. Soon I, too, knew how to play the child's game. I learned well how to gather up my toys and run away.

• • •

They did not look like a promising pair, these two fellows with a day's growth of beard and a bottle of Southern Comfort perched between them. Lazing on the front stoop near a big, old pickup with shotguns loaded in back, they had the look of strangers I'd met before, strangers who might get overly friendly as the night wore on and the contents of their bottle dwindled down. Since their room in this sad one-story motel in a sad central Louisiana town was separated from mine by a lock that looked mostly cosmetic, I drew the line swiftly, dropping off my bag and quickly climbing back into my car. Pulling out, I gave them a breezy wave. Just to let them know I was neither interested nor intimidated.

These are the kinds of nights on the road when I think about the fact that no one knows quite where I am. They are the nights in strange outposts in unfamiliar states when the world starts to feel large and creepy, my place in it tentative and very small. If I'm feeling maudlin and have the time, I start to muse on what would happen if I were simply to disappear. How long would it take before friends and family figured out that I was actually gone? Fortunately, perhaps because I've got a reporter's notebook as an excuse, these are also the nights when I start conversations with strangers who unfailingly have something to share. All at once, I am not the least bit alone.

It was balmy in Coushatta, Louisiana, the air full of a musky scent I couldn't quite identify. There were only a few places open for dinner. I chose the most welcoming, a brightly lit Mexican joint with plastic tablecloths and no pretense about serving ethnic cuisine. Celebrating diversity didn't appear to be high on the agenda around town. From what I could tell, segregation was as firmly a part of the landscape as the Red River soil. Black women shopped at an overpriced mini-mart up the street, bordering the "bad" side of town. Down closer to the bank and the Piggly Wiggly was an airy cafe favored by the sheriff and relatively prosperous looking white men in bright-colored sports shirts. Paula and Ismael Rodriguez's place fell somewhere in between. They made me some spicy enchiladas, which I ate while we shot the breeze for awhile. It hadn't been easy, they said, opening a Mexican restaurant in a town whose lines had been drawn generations back. Too often too many of their tables were empty.

"Sometimes it does get to you and you wonder what you're doing wrong. You wonder what more to do, but it all works out," said Rodriguez, twenty-seven, who had emigrated north at the age of fourteen in search of a better life. He had a wife now and two young children. He was a businessman and homeowner.

"I'm close now," he said when I asked if he was satisfied. "We don't need much. Maybe next year there will be enough." Maybe someday he would have money enough to send back to his hometown in Mexico, where they badly needed a park. When he got on his feet, Rodriguez said, it would be nice to give the kids there someplace to play. It was one of the things that he'd longed for growing up. His Anglo wife, Paula, who had been clearing dishes at a table nearby, stopped and smiled as if she were hearing him speak of his childhood for the first time. "We'll get your dream," she said, then shooed their nine-year-old son off into the kitchen.

Inevitably, it grew late and it was time to go home, or to what was home on this particular night; back to the flimsy strip of motel rooms where my friends were sitting just as I'd left them, tipped back in metal chairs set out on the cement stoop between our neighboring plywood front doors. I did not want to chat.

"Nice night," said the guy with the thick mustache.

"Sure is," I said, putting my key in the door.

"No, really," said his friend. "Stop a minute. Just take a look."

Reluctantly I did, turning around to see a stage-set sliver of moon suspended between the sinews of an ancient pecan tree beside the dusty state road several yards away. I took a deep breath, felt my shoulders loosen a little.

"We've been out rabbit hunting all day," said the mustache, whose named turned out to be J. L. Shilling. "We've got that good kind of tired."

Soon I'd dragged a chair out of my room and planted myself beside them. Soon these two guys who had looked like trouble began to look instead like what they were: a couple of family men enjoying the evening air. I'd come to Coushatta to report a story that ultimately never panned out. But during that same period several years ago, I was also deep into a project for which everyone was a potential interview: a series about the search for happiness that preoccupies so many people in America.

And so I asked J. L. Shilling and his buddy, Thomas Hopkins, were they happy?

"My parents were uneducated people who didn't expect much—a clean home, clean clothes, a decent vehicle to ride in and church on Sundays," said Shilling, who at fifty-three was retired after twenty-five years of working for Louisiana's state department of transportation. He'd been married thirty-four years, had two grown children and a belly full of barbecued ribs purchased at a local pit. "My parents didn't expect much, so of course they were happy. A day's work for a day's pay. . . . It's funny, isn't it, all this racing around full speed ahead, trying this, then trying that?"

J. L. Shilling wasn't sure what exactly had changed, but somehow in the shift from his parents' generation to his own to his children's and grandchildren's, the measure of happiness had fundamentally altered. One change, he said, was that happiness had come to be measured at all. There were polls taken and books written about it, talk shows dissecting it and businesses capitalizing on it. The ideal was no longer something you prayed for in the next world. It was a birthright to which people felt entitled in the here-and-now.

"Come down to earth," he said, chuckling. "We've lost touch with reality."

What you've got, J. L. Shilling said, extending his big cowboy boots toward the curb, is "a whole lot of people who aren't ever gonna be fulfilled because they're full-speed ahead trying to achieve something that's not there. That's how they do in New York, wouldn't you say? Don't know your neighbors. No easy way to relax. If I had to go home every night to a tenth-story apartment, I'd just smash my head against the wall."

I did not live in a tenth-story "CEE-ment block," as he later called it. My apartment was on the twelfth floor, which in real estate calculus was something better but now seemed only worse. Suddenly I was acutely aware that the only thing green and growing in my home was a pathetic rubber tree I'd found early one morning on Columbus Avenue, slumped like a spurned lover near a pile of trash. I could hear the blare of low-level city noise that seeped even into my bedroom late at night all those twelve stories up. Sitting there in the still silence that evening in Louisiana, for all the excitement and joyous cacophony I'd loved in New York, I felt, too, all the precious energy that the battle in living there claimed. Shilling and his wife made their home on a river near a sandbar where they could fish after dinner. When his beagle hounds wanted out, he'd open the back door and let them run. In Manhattan, where I'd been living for the past two years, pet therapists and doggy day care were the new craze.

J. L. Shilling laughed when I told him this. He could not quite fathom the world that I lived in, and on that sultry night, neither could I. "I don't know," he said. "Happiness is simple. Why do so many people make it so hard?"

I was nodding now, agreeing with him, but at the same moment a whole series of faces flashed through my head: I saw Paula Soto, a promising teacher-to-be who was murdered by a stray bullet while out practicing on a Bronx field with her college softball team; the out-of-work Illinois clothing salesman, a father who could not be a provider, whom I'd met in a bar two days after his mortgage payment was due; the drug-addicted young man who once asked if he could come along on my travels because, well, he had nowhere else to go. I knew life wasn't anything close to as simple as what Shilling described.

Yet, inexorably, I also knew that it did not have to be as complicated as many of us make it.

I'd been talking for months with people dead-set on acquiring happiness, almost as if it were a commodity that actually could be owned. I'd talked to people dissatisfied with their bodies, their jobs, their spouses, their neighbors, their scaled-back dreams. There were generalizations I could make and issues I could define, legitimate frustrations and all manner of good intentions to be found among citizens groping toward fulfillment. But not all of it would fit tidily into the three-part newspaper series I intended to write.

And on that balmy night in Coushatta, Louisiana, I realized why. The search was about something both splendidly basic and hopelessly abstract:

At the heart of America's compulsive search for happiness was a longing for home.

• • •

There is a man you should know, a guy whose life describes what adulthood means.

I knew him at first mainly because my apartment building in Manhattan was adjacent to the spot where he kept regular hours, begging roughly from 8 to 3. Around lunchtime he would break, leaning up against a wall to eat an egg sandwich or banana or whatever else he had scrounged. Sometimes he read yesterday's funnies, fished from a trash bin, or waved at passengers on the M86 bus as, in a cloud of soot, it roared by. If the morning had gone particularly badly, or well, he'd quit a bit early and head for the liquor store four blocks down. I knew this much of William Bell Jr. before I knew even his name.

Like most New Yorkers, I struggled daily with the

mini moral dilemmas evoked by a barrage of beggars' faces and, like most New Yorkers, I had balanced thousands of quick, brutal equations. This one is clearly aggressive, probably on drugs. Steer clear. This one has on some pretty sharp-looking running shoes. No dice. But wait, think twice. What if she just lost her job? What if she's fleeing an abusive husband? Drop some spare change, at least. This one has a dog. Go on, give him a dollar. It was hopeless, like trying to gage human indignity through the reflection in a funhouse mirror, for I knew that the one with the dog was probably the worst shyster of all. In the end, I mostly went on gut and the look in each man or woman's eye. If nothing else, no matter how little my small handouts were worth, it seemed important to do at least that.

In Bell's eyes I saw a smooth operator, but thought I'd also just barely glimpsed something more. And so one day I stopped and asked if he would let me make him the subject of a story about panhandling. He said that I could. I asked if he could meet me at his corner the next day at 4 o'clock. He said that he would, though I doubted that he'd actually show up. The thing about William Bell Jr., though, was that he did show up and continued to do so over the weeks that followed. Not only that, but he never asked me for money or told me a story that didn't check out. Though he was an addict, and addicts aren't known for their reliability, and though he was down, and Bell was pretty damned down, he kept to a code. There were certain things he would not do, and giving the run-around to hapless reporters was apparently one of them.

Our first extended conversation was over hamburgers at the Three-Star Diner, a few paces back from the newspaper kiosk and over from the bus stop on Bell's corner. He was reserved, a little awkward under the eyes of waitresses and cashiers who knew him as a charity case, not a customer. "I used to watch 'Donna Reed' and 'Father Knows Best' as a kid growing up," said Bell, who was then forty-one. "That was the life I was going to get when I grew up. That's what I wanted, to settle down in a nice house." Life could not have unfolded any further from his picket-fenced dream. His mother had five children with several different men and his father was heavily into both dealing and using cocaine, which "killed him in the end. Just corroded his bones til there was nothing much left."

In his teens, partly to escape the turmoil and partly to find himself, Bell joined the military. "The Marines. It had to be the Marines, because I wanted to be with the best." Quickly he found himself in Vietnam, facing the worst, making his first real acquaintances with terror and prejudice and death. It was a bumpy passage and when William Bell Jr. came home, it was to a nation torn apart. He sought solace with an old girlfriend, who bore him a daughter and became his wife. He had a job painting houses. Soon he'd had a whole series of jobs, all of them lost because he also had a whole lot of attitude, a whole lot of anger. In time, when his wife, Deborah, had had enough, his marriage went too. Ties with family frayed, his list of crashpads got thinner, his addictions grew ever more serious as Bell tried to blot out the confusion and pain. All at once, it seemed, a quarter century—more than half of his life—had passed in a blur on the streets.

"So that's my story," he said, jogging me back to the diner's din. "Pretty sorry, huh? Pretty typical."

Bell's was a not an atypical street person's story. It was the way he told it, not with perfect grammar or fancy words, but in a cadence so lyrical and absorbing that, to my horror, when he was done I looked down at my notebook and realized I'd scrawled only a few partial quotes.

After that, we always kept a tape recorder nearby.

I guess the same special something that I found in William many of my neighbors found as well. Though doubtless well-practiced at averting their eyes from the beggars clotted at subway stairwells or near banking machines, people on the Upper West Side gave to him freely and in very personal ways. They brought food from their dinner tables and gifts during the holidays, clothing when it was cold and a steady stream of cash. They stopped so Bell could kneel down and josh with their children. When he'd go missing for a few days or more, they would inquire about him at the newsstand. "What it is, well, it's like a feeling I got here. I'm comfortable on this corner.... I know a lot of people care," Bell told me the first time we had lunch. He knew this was no kind of life, but as life on the streets went, it wasn't half-bad. And so he stayed, selling off chunks of his self-respect for the price of a pint of Thunderbird or a little crack cocaine. It was a miserable existence. The winter months, especially, were harsh. And over time it was clear that he was deteriorating, reduced sometimes to drunkenly flailing at random passing cars. Few could look at him without wincing; few could pass by without dropping a few cents in his cup.

"People want to help, and that's understandable," Ruby Bove, a veteran counselor at St. Christopher's Inn, an upstate New York shelter, told me in an interview for my story about Bell, "but all it does is make it easy for them to stay on the streets. It keeps them from helping themselves. It's killing them slowly with kindness."

After researching my story, I never again felt the same about giving panhandlers money, when I gave money at all. This is how more and more people are feeling, and the fact that advocates for the homeless frequently take a stand similar to Ruby Bove's provides a rationale that eases much of the guilt. But even after my article was done and published, even though I now knew it would do no good to give Bell money, he was still there, standing in the same unhappy place. It was obvious that if he didn't get off the streets, he would die. "Living out here starts to wear on you, body and soul," he said one evening. "I got to make a change." I didn't know quite what to do anymore so, dropping all pretense of being the objective journalist, I started making some calls.

There were shelters ready to take him and people ready to help, but more was required. Time and again, Bell had headed off for a program and days later ended up back at his corner. He called himself a T. C. bum—a Therapeutic Community bum. Over and over, there had been disappointment on all sides. "I was really rooting for him," Monsy Rodrigues, a waitress at the Three-Star Diner, said after once glimpsing Bell clean-shaven and dried out. "He was looking so good, all cleaned up like that. Now I know he can do for himself, but he doesn't. He'd rather be standing on the corner. Back where he is."

This remained true for a time. But it was hard to give up on Bell because Bell himself never did. Something in him, however erratic, kept holding on.

We are stunned now in looking back. It has been four years since Bell left the streets for good. Each time I speak with him goosebumps run up my arms. Miles from Manhattan, he lives today in upstate Albany, where he has a job selling shoes at Walmart, health insurance and support groups, a house that he happily shares with Joan, a good woman whom he soon plans to marry. He has reconciled with his family, made peace with the grown daughter he never knew and amends with her mother. Most of all, he has found a steady, deep faith and, for the first time in his life, a strong sense of home.

"We have the everyday problems, you know, the bills and things like that," he said recently. "But I come from a cardboard box in Central Park. I never forget that. And now I have my house with the white picket fence. I have me a whole entire home, with cable TV. Ain't that somethin'? Ain't that *somethin'*."

When we've tried to figure how Bell did it, how he beat the incredible odds, we unsurprisingly find no easy explanation. Two things, though, come up again and again. The first perhaps was simply a blessing: He always had his code, an abiding, baseline morality that surely would have crumbled eventually had he remained on the streets. The second was the strange way in which on 86th Street he found the beginnings of something like home. "I'd totally cut myself off from life. I was just a nomad out there, doing what I had to to survive," he said over a lunch of fried chicken and coldcuts Joan prepared one snowy afternoon before Christmas. What finally made the difference, he said, was the sense that there were people who cared and weren't going to stop. With each baby step he took, at each program he tried, from everyone he met, Bell snagged bits of strength—the kind of strength given by people willing to stand by. People like Shirley Gibbs-Bryant, an overworked social worker whose clients sometimes came from the Salvation Army shelter in suburban New York where Bell stayed for a time. When he needed drug treatment, she tracked down a facility that could spare a bed. When he dropped out of sight, she got into her car and drove down from her home in Mt. Vernon to search the city's streets. She did not let him go.

Bell's road wound around many bends and turned back on itself many times. But Gibbs-Bryant and a small band of others kept the faith, believed in Bell unconditionally and firmly enough that in time, somehow, Bell came to believe in himself. He took charge, finally got a grip. He gave up the excuses.

"I finally got tired of blaming, blaming, blaming. It's about accepting responsibility for yourself as a person. I finally got off my ass and made some commitments. *Commitment* is what it's about," he said recently. "It's not even about love. It's about being committed to helping ourselves and each other, man to a woman, parent to child. Not just saying you're committed, but *doing* it. Doing it every day."

A year or so ago I was walking west on 86th Street when in the distance, seated on the edge of an overstuffed trash can, I spotted the silhouette of a man wearing a beard and baseball cap. My stomach jerked. Drawing closer, I could see that his eyes were cast down. He looked defeated, as he had after flunking out of rehab programs in the past. It had been about six weeks since Bell and I had been in contact, but I'd been resting easy. Though the rate of relapse among drug addicts is high, he had seemed so at peace with the counsel and supportive community in upstate New York. What disappointment could have brought him to this? Then suddenly I knew. I knew it was AIDS. He'd tested HIV positive some years earlier, before ever leaving the streets. Now it was full blown, and in turmoil he'd given up. Drawing closer still, I saw his cheeks, hollow, and his eyes, a little bit wild. A few yards more and we were face to face, me lost in panic and disappointment. I looked up.

It wasn't Bell.

I nearly cried. The guy said he was hungry, so I went upstairs and fixed him something to eat, knowing he'd probably toss the sandwiches and fruit, keeping perhaps the brownie and can of soda. I didn't care. I handed the

William Bell Jr. leaving work, Christmastime, 1995, in Albany, New York.

stranger his dinner, then rushed back upstairs to dial Albany, finding William Bell Jr. at home. Over the next hour we talked about his life, my life, the subject of this book. He had become such a wonderful man, so strong and purposeful and clear eyed, living by example, caring for others around him as much as he cared for himself. By now I was feeling pretty guilty about ever having doubted his commitment to this new life. But he was touched when I confessed what had happened earlier in the evening.

"That means something to me, that you still think about me when you cross that street. You're still looking out, and I appreciate that," he said. We talked for a while about what he thought had truly made the difference and again he said it was commitment. Finally, he had understood that "it's easy to throw trash on the street, to sleep with a woman, to sit around and complain, take all the time without givin' a thought to givin'."

What's hard, he said, is keeping things clean.

I think what he meant was that whether you're bending over to pick up a piece of trash on the street or taking time to help a person in trouble, whether you're comfortable and well-off or poor and down on your luck, the measure of success lies in self-respect. It takes dignity and character to do the right things.

"If you're so into money or greed or lookin' out for yourself, if all you can think of is *gettin' me mine* while this neighbor is hurting or that baby is runnin' naked down the street—if that's what you're about—you're miserable. A person who doesn't know how to give—I don't care if that person's rich or poor or black or white—if that person can't look outside himself, then he's feelin' worthless. There are a whole lotta people out there feelin' worthless. We got a whole big part of society with no commitments to anything but gettin' me mine. Even people with morals and values, they're lookin' to get theirs, to get this thing—the American dream," Bell said, agitation in his voice. "But, you see, we got no dreams. If we got no commitments, we got no dreams."

Today, most of the time, Bell's old spot on 86th Street is occupied by Tony, a scraggly white guy who looks sixty, but says he's nearer to fifty and looks older each day. I hear the skinny woman called Lisa, who was a corner regular for awhile, is in jail again. The last time I saw the woman known as "Lisa's sister," she looked very pregnant and very strung out. Smokey, a puffy-fingered crack addict who was also a fixture in the neighborhood for a long time, is dead.

Not all of these people could or would have wanted to be helped. Certainly many are already too far gone. But there is something equally as certain, something that I'll never again doubt: the only sure failure is in refusing to look around for ways to reach out. The only unforgivable sin is in caring so much for our own personal comfort that all sight of that old-fashioned obligation called service is irretrievably lost. When at first we met, I had no idea that William Bell Jr. would become an enduring friend. Now, when I think of life without him, it seems as blank as the faces of all those in pain whom we blankly walk by.

"Today, God has given me a chance to be William, to live by morals that were on the back burner when I was out on the streets. I'm my own man. I'm a doer today. I'm my own person. I am William. And I love William today," Bell told me the last time I visited Albany. "I care for myself. I care for other people. That makes me a man, a person. That makes me a part of somethin' real, somethin' I worked for and earned. And I didn't do it alone. What helped me leave that corner was having a feeling of home, a family there on that corner of mine."

On his panhandler's corner, Bell began to grow up. On his panhandler's corner, he found the tender beginnings of an American dream.

2 Getting Real
Facing the Fact That You Can't Have It All

When I was a kid, maybe six or seven years old, my grandfather proposed a stunning, eye-popping gift. "Go ahead," he said, letting his grandchildren loose in one of the world's largest toy stores. "You may choose whatever you wish." It should be said that, when it came to child rearing, my parents weren't into buying us a lot of "stuff." Theirs was more a "use-your-imagination" esthetic (in its own way a tremendous gift). So it was that on the day I was left to roam among all those aisles of playthings I had my first glimpse at a character trait that dogs me to this day.

At first, I was elated. So much possibility! Then trouble set in.

At first, I strolled leisurely here and there, happily exploring my options. Maybe a china doll or something by Madame Alexander? No, too frou-frou. Well, then, what about a badminton set? Hell no, a playmate would be required. Fine. What about a puzzle or chemistry set? Too educational. Go on. Go for it. Just look at that kid-sized electric car! Far too extravagant. As I wandered back and forth, the overstuffed shelves grew taller and anxiety edged in. By now the other grandchildren had contentedly settled on their choices, a stuffed animal or model airplane or I don't remember what, while I was still trapped. I could go in this direction, but what about that?

Finally, far too many hours later, according to the family lore, I settled somewhat wretchedly on a Mr. Rogers songbook (friends taunt me to this day for not having at least made a run at the electric car). The thing was, it didn't matter anymore what I chose, so relieved was I that the choosing was done. Possibility had overwhelmed me and what started out as a kindness had turned into a curse.

Sometimes when I think about America and the many people I've met, I wonder if this isn't part of our own paralysis. Perhaps so many of us have been given so much, had so many decades of unparalleled expansion and opportunity, that now—faced with tough choices—we just want it all to go away. Certainly if you talk with older people, they'll tell you as much. Growing up in the Depression, you didn't waste a lot of time pondering your wounded inner child, questing for a glamorous hard body or trading in your imperfect spouse. You didn't labor over real or imagined slights or could-have-hads. Expectations were different. Indulgence simply wasn't a standard option back then.

To much of the world, we in the United States look like amazingly spoiled children, the ugly image only compounded by the sniveling we do despite all the wealth. It's grown to be part of our culture, the new culture of victimization. Blame me? Well sue you! The more reflexive these responses become, the more painful—even unthinkable—it becomes to choose responsibility, which after all is about as bland and unsexy as a Mr. Rogers songbook.

So two young men named Menendez brutally murder their parents and build an abuse defense persuasive enough to hang two juries. A black man opens fire on a packed New York commuter train and it is explained as an act of cumulative black rage. A woman slices off her husband's penis and is excused because she was the victim of domestic violence. All these defenses bear consideration, for each represents legitimate and serious torment with real psychological ramifications. Child abuse, racism and domestic violence are shamefully common in America. But there is also the old idea that two wrongs don't make a right, that ultimately each of us is accountable for the choices we make, whatever the circumstances. Civil society depends on some adherence to a morality, to the notions of righteousness and personal responsibility even in the face of tremendous pain.

It was perhaps an ugly twist on this instinct that prompted nods of support from many around the country when Singapore issued an American teenager convicted of vandalism four painful strokes with a bamboo cane. Some denounced the lashing as a human rights violation, decrying it as unreasonably harsh. But a substantial number of people took a different view, applauding the reprisal. Talk-radio waves were filled with voices cheering the law-and-order message. Legislators in several states proposed a similar system be adopted to combat deviancy at home. Even those who winced at the primitivism of it all pondered whether some public humiliation and physical suffering might not be exactly the sort of retribution America's criminals need and deserve.

For my part, it's been a long time since that fateful toy store fiasco. But in many ways I've remained that girl, up there with the best of them when it comes to making excuses and ducking hard choices as best I can. Since leaving my northern California home fifteen years ago, I have lived at sixteen different addresses in a zigzag path extending from New York to Rhode Island to Washington, D.C., from Paris, France, to Indianapolis, Indiana. From Boston to New York to Boston and back again. All the while doubling back on myself internally as well. Part good girl, part bad girl, from church on Sunday to the Irish bar around the block. From too many cigarettes and too much wine on Friday to teaching at-risk kids on Saturday. From late nights at jazz clubs and tempestuous romances to long stretches of quiet, solo contemplation. One minute chasing after an earthquake or war, the next imagining a blessed life in the country. Back and forth.

Then back again.

But the fact is that I'm an adult and around the time I turned thirty some common sense finally kicked in. It finally dawned on me that however many choices lay at our feet, it is important finally just to make one. Get in the game. Show some gumption, for God's sake, and let relief flood in. It may be that things could be different, that there are other routes to take, but the reality is we are ultimately about the choices we make—or fail to make—every single day.

• • •

Early one morning an AP colleague in New York called to say that a dear friend had been found dead, jackknifed over a tin of food he was opening for a cat he'd always pretended to hate. He was barely past fifty. He should be around today. That he isn't is in no small measure his own fault: He'd drunk too much and smoked too many cigarettes, never caring particularly about the long view. He led with his heart, which was part of his charm.

And the shame.

I was miles away when he died, relishing San Francisco's choppy bay and muted headlands, the bridges and four-lane highways whose curves were so smooth, so familiar. This was where I'd grown up, a slice of the world whose incomparable beauty I'd abandoned without a thought at the age of seventeen. Now, a little more than a decade later, the landscape soothed me as nothing could.

I'd come to California for a weekend retreat at Esalen, the granddaddy of all human potential centers. It was research for my series on America's obsessive pursuit of happiness. But in truth I'd also been intrigued in a personal way. Maybe as a bonus I would acquire some tidbit of Zen-inspired wisdom for myself.

Now, though, my friend was dead and nothing else seemed much to matter. I'd lost my stomach for New-Age introspection. I had not the least interest in listening to people ponder their "inner children" and couldn't stomach the thought of examining mine. I had no interest in talking or listening, to anyone or anything at all.

As I wound along Highway 1 toward Big Sur, transfixed by a sense of being at the continent's edge, I grew progressively more detached. Each breathtaking vista seemed only to distract, so much so that I nearly missed the low-key road sign. All at once, I'd reached Esalen and grudgingly checked in. My assigned bunkmate was a woman who had come alone, she said, to resolve some confusion about her foundering marriage. Like me, she did not feel much like talking, though on our second night I saw her huddled in intent conversation with a mustachioed man. After that, I never saw her again. Unpacking my bag, I wondered what had possessed me to propose this trip. A native of California and a product of the '70s, I was at best skeptical of the human potential movement. While the nuns at my Catholic girls school were preaching self-sacrifice, self-centeredness had seemed more the ethos of the day. I'd seen it creep in and cleave apart too many families, watched too many adults suddenly start acting like children. This was what I was thinking about as I left my bungalow to head down toward the sea. Bird song followed me along the dirt path. Monarch butterflies clogged the cyprus and acacia trees. The scent of eucalyptus suffused everything. It was the scent of my childhood home.

That first night I ate dinner alone, out on a deck, while somewhere nearby I could hear tom-toms and primal screams. I smiled to myself. Esalen was a tranquil place, but incredibly odd. I read a John Steinbeck novel over my vegetarian lentil stew and, without a single interview done, went off to bed. There was no smoking, nor a bar.

Tomorrow, I vowed, the reporting would begin in earnest.

"What we're going to do now is create a bliss grid," said our workshop leader as a group of about a dozen adults gathered in a cabin early the next morning. By now we all had our shoes off and were seated in a circle. Everyone knew that I was a reporter, but agreed to overlook that fact. And so, as instructed, we began making lists of things we liked, things we were curious about, things that we wished never to experience again. In my notes now I see scrawled in raggedy block letters a list not terribly different from one I might make today.

Things I like: "Central Park early Sunday morning. Sibelius and Saint Saens. Great conversation. Mediterranean food. Choirs at church on Sunday. Being in unlikely places."

Things I'm curious about: "Bugs—so I won't be afraid. How to fly a plane. Traveling the world carrying only a sack. Nicotine addiction. How to become a good public speaker. Art history. Religion. Gardening."

Things I never want to do again: "Pay rent. Have a hangover. Move. Break up with a boyfriend. Feel isolated among a group of friends or colleagues. Watch a friend die. Be unable to hear my heart."

We shared our lists, explored and debated each other's ideas. Eventually we were asked to lie down (how I hated this part!) and spend some time doing what our leader called visualization. She began by telling us to relax, which only made me want to giggle. But slowly, as time went along, her voice became a sort of lullaby. And I could see myself in the perfect place she asked us to imagine. I could see myself in a cottage by the water, playing the piano and writing in longhand. I could smell garlic-laden eggplant stew on the stove, feel the gentle night air as I roamed my small vegetable garden making friends with even the most despicable bugs. By the time we broke for dinner, I'd been transported.

Maybe there was something to this sort of deliberate self-searching. Maybe it was possible to list, then clarify, then envision an ideal path through life's pandemonium. Even if I was only half sold, it was an emboldening thought.

Not long after dawn on my second day, I summoned nerve enough to head down to Esalen's informal trademark, the communal hot tubs whose raciness I'd heard about as a kid. Adults—people our *parents*' age—had gone there and—*gasp!*—sat buck naked together. It was the zenith of touchy-feeliness and, to say the least, not my kind of thing. But I persuaded myself that it was somehow essential to reporting my story and so, trailing a white terry-cloth towel, I toddled off toward the bathhouse and, with a determined air of insouciance, dropped my towel and climbed into a tub. Soon it began to fill with early risers and, like me, a few bashful others hoping to dodge peak-hour crowds. It was quiet at first, a handful of bathers contemplating the ribbon of fog stretched along the Pacific shoreline far below. Grownups wearing no more than a wristwatch, sloshing about like awkward, overgrown children.

At length, Bather No. 1, in a salt-and-pepper beard with a sizable belly and hair on his back, turned to Bather No. 2, a Rubenesque blonde with freckled thighs, unshaved armpits and a New Age crystal dangling from her neck.

"This is definitely heaven," said the guy, who had driven up from Hollywood to recharge his batteries. "But I don't like to call it that."

For an instant, the woman looked baffled. Then her eyes widened and her head began to bob in recognition: "Ohhh," she trilled. "I know what you mean. When you come expecting heaven, things always fall short."

An uneasy silence followed, broken only by the barking of sea lions at play in the surf far below. Their cries were a taunt: "See how easy it is? See how easy it can be? Look here. *This* is happiness."

But evolution had played a nasty trick. Those of us in that hot tub, and in so many metaphorical hot tubs all across the nation, were living in a world that had grown incredibly complex—so complex that simplicity had somehow become one of the things hardest to find. Looking around at my well-meaning companions that morning, I thought of what our Depression-era parents and grandparents might have had to say.

For us, food on the table and a stiff upper lip were not enough. Women had to have equal rights, gays and minorities their civil rights. Drugs had promised higher consciousness and the sexual revolution had promised freedom from outmoded Victorian conventions. Though many in America had not identified with the college students who marched against Vietnam or participated in the counter-cultural rock festival known as Woodstock, though the phenomenon we now call "The Sixties" had not personally touched everyone, neither had anyone escaped. The nation was changed by an era some believe was full of necessary bounds-breaking discovery and others define as the sorry sacrifice of the nation's most basic values.

As the pitch of protest subsided in the mid-1970s, the years went along, the streets quieted. But the pursuit of something, of that thing that would feel stronger and truer, grew no less intense. The anger and hunger were not gone. They were only reshaped, redefined. Now bodies would be beautiful and psyches thoroughly actualized. People would have "significant others" instead of mates, "challenges" instead of handicaps, "convenient shopping" instead of mom-and-pop stores, "fulfilling careers" instead of jobs. The Declaration of Independence may have guaranteed a right to the pursuit of happiness. But the stakes had been ratcheted higher, then higher still. Happiness was not something merely to be chased. It was out there just waiting to be grabbed.

And so we have looked, stumbling doggedly toward the magic potion, the promotion or product or pastime that might make us feel good, then better, then best. We've locked ourselves into an ever more intricate game of hide-and-seek, devoted millions of dollars and as many hours to getting all that we deserve.

And in a way, maybe we have gotten just that.

The deficit now has passed three trillion dollars. Our homes, schools, community institutions and infrastructure are in disrepair. Children kill children, parents abandon each other, towns lack committed citizens. None of it happened overnight. Sort of like the ten pounds that one day just seem to show up on the scale, the way we perceive ourselves and the expectations we carry have evolved gradually, over time. "Unfortunately, we have been expecting the glass to be full, so when the water doesn't go all the way to the top, we think it's empty. Maybe it's better to start with the notion that there will be no water at all. My children never knew the hardships we went through during the war," Mihaly Csikszentmihalyi, a Hungarian psychologist who was in Italy during World War II, told me some time ago from his office at the University of Chicago. "We've had in this country a kind of innocent, naive notion about letting it all hang out, the playboy philosophy that somehow sex, youth and money was going to make us happy.... But it's nonsense. It's nowhere written that we should have all that. Most people eventually realize that life is basically a hard job."

Life is hard. It is an obvious notion. This was firm in my mind as I sat with strangers in a hot tub perched on the edge of California. My friend was dead, had died too young. But we kept on looking, scanning the horizon for happiness, while the sea lions played in the bubbling surf far below.

• • •

There is in the dream of America a sense of promise, the idea that we can make something of ourselves and in so doing make something far grander, a whole country full of prosperity and possibility, a place where diverse individuals thrive in union. What we keep banging up against is a more complicated reality. Maybe that's why I love New York cabdrivers. However grumpy their dispositions or broken their English might be, they get to the point. No bull.

Some of the most lucid, direct, realistic conversations I've had about America's fate have been held from the Naugahyde backseats of yellow taxis speeding to somewhere. Maybe it's all the travelers they meet, the frank confessions they hear from people who place cabbies among the ranks of bartenders, therapists and priests. Perhaps it's all the talk they hear on their AM dial, or the opportunity for prolonged meditation in the stop-and-go monotony of rush-hour traffic. Whatever the reasons, more often than not, it has taken a taxi driver to crystallize in a few blunt words the concerns and mood of people I've spoken with at length all around the nation. There was, for instance, the Romanian whose name I didn't get. Simply, poignantly, he captured something that many of us frequently fail to see.

It was early morning, early enough that I had to blink hard once settled inside his spotless sedan. The upholstery shone like freshly buffed silver, the interior smelled of pine and from the back of the front seat hung a magazine rack for passengers' reading pleasure. It was unlike any taxi I'd ever been in before. And the man who drove it, a curly-haired thirty-nine-year-old father of two, clearly was proud of it.

As we made our way over the Triborough Bridge toward LaGuardia Airport, he shared with me the progress of his young family. They'd arrived in America five years before with next to nothing. His wife and children, who spoke no English, had found leaving the land of their birth a huge jolt. For his part, the Romanian had been well educated and doing all right back home, but he had wanted something better for his children. He wanted them to grow up in an open, even exuberant democracy. He wanted them to have a boundless future, even if for now his own would be limited. Trying feebly to offer a little encouragement, I suggested that things could only look up, that the nation had gone through unusually hard times in the early '90s, what with the recession and all. In the rearview mirror I saw his eyes grow wide.

"Use that word carefully," he said, not the least preachy. "People here don't know hard. They've been spoiled. *Hard* isn't a real word in America."

These five years, he said, had been the best of his life.

It's not that Americans don't appreciate all this country has to offer. It's more like we just forget to remember a lot of the time. We're frustrated, disappointed, preoccupied by our personal worlds. Thomas Ingaglio, a cabbie who drove me out to Newark Airport not long ago, chimed in on this topic. He was mad as hell about the fact that cars were being stolen every night in his middle-class Bronx neighborhood. Years ago, when he was a young man, residents hadn't even bothered to lock the doors to their homes. Today even the most elaborate alarm systems failed to keep robbers away. "There's no fear anymore—not of your father, God, your schoolteachers. Not of the law, or even shame," said the lifelong New Yorker and Korean War vet. "The little guy is squeezed, trapped on all sides. Common sense. That's what we lost. You gotta have common sense."

Still, he said as we cruised through Lincoln Tunnel, "to get back to the brighter side, I tell my kids there is no place in the world like this city, this country. You won't find all the cultures and excitement anywhere else. The lowest guy on the street can work himself up and make something of his life. You can make things happen if you want to bad enough."

"It's the government," said Jesus Munoz, a well-spoken driver who, like Ingaglio, was in middle age. He was driving me back from Kennedy Airport one Saturday night after I'd apparently missed a stunning spring day, shards of which I'd glimpsed as Flight #233 from Nashville descended on the city's sharp, electric sunset skyline. He started to elaborate on his beef with politicians, then suddenly paused. "No. I don't mean that exactly. It's not the government," Munoz said. "It's us. It's the people. We are the government. That's the way the democratic idea is supposed to work."

Stopped at a red light on the edge of Harlem, a glassy-eyed black man approached the cab. Munoz, dignified, even sympathetic, reluctantly dug into his pocket and handed over some change. "We don't speak up. We aren't protecting this thing, the American dream. All these years it has taken us to figure out that giving people money without giving them work doesn't help anyone. And the media. We need media that educates the people. It's communication. That's how you make things work. But today we are all separated in our own sad little worlds."

Jesus Munoz was quiet a while, perhaps thinking back to the promise that drew him to adopt this country as his home decades before. He had not lost faith. "Things will get better," he said as we sped down Columbus Avenue, past people of all colors and classes strolling among bodegas and neon-lit cafes, masses of people living close together and far more peacefully than the nightly news would have anyone believe.

"We are like a very rich man who is suddenly broke. At first, yes, it's very hard. He is down and out, depressed. But then he realizes all he can do, all the ideas and creativity he has in him. And new life flows from this knowing. He starts over again and is only wiser this time," said Munoz, his poetry giving me a chill. "We need leaders to show the way, yes. But leaders are led by the people. The people must lead leaders. We have to speak up, find ways to come back together. It will happen, I think, because the crime, the sadness, the depression now has hit us all."

We are as a nation, he said, "the rich man who is not so rich anymore."

• • •

One afternoon I pulled off the highway into Newcomerstown, Ohio, where I stopped to see legendary pitcher Cy Young's childhood home and feed my rental car some gas. But just as I'd paid up and was ready to go, a conversation got started and before long a whole extended gas station family had gathered around. There was Pam Greathouse, thirty-nine, the manager and a mother of three, and her younger husband, Milo Bund, twenty-three, with whom she worked and now shared a son. A mechanic, second cashier and small peanut gallery of friends rounded out the group. It was an animated crowd. But were they a community, I wondered aloud? Did they feel they belong? Well, yes and no, they said, then explained why.

"If you're low-income, you're trash. Nothing. That's how you feel," said Amy Kinkade, who had stopped by for some gas and to shoot the breeze. "There are the people who run things—they're the high and mighty—and then there's the rest of us. It's that way everywhere. There's two or three people who own the whole town."

"You know," said John Hough, 41, a friend and part-time attendant at the gas station, "we're so used to that mentality. It's like minding your parents. It's a mindset. You're stuck."

"It's like a never-ending black hole," added Bund.

"It's like nobody wants to get involved," said Ms. Kinkade.

"Yeah," Hough continued, "but if all the low-income people marched on Washington and said, 'Hey, we're tired of working for $4.25 and paying $2.50 for a gallon of milk. Well, you wonder what would happen. It all comes down to people. We're gonna have to work together."

"You hang in because of your children. You want them to do better than you did. You try to give your child some hope," said Greathouse, who faded in and out between customers. "Even if it's a pipe dream."

Bund and Greathouse had at this point consigned themselves to a week-to-week existence, working side-by-side and splitting the pocket change. They were not unlike a lot of people, struggling somewhere toward the bottom of their town's social food chain. The pretty gabled houses weren't theirs, nor had they ever toured around the hallowed little museum kept in Cy Young's memory just a few blocks away. They didn't have much education or any real mobility. They were doing the best they could, but they knew it wasn't enough. They wanted a sense of family, but weren't even quite sure what that had come to mean.

Greathouse echoed other parents I have known when she told a little story about what had happened after she had spanked her three-year-old son one day a few weeks back. He'd promptly toddled over to his plastic kiddie phone, picked up the make-believe receiver and dialed. He pretended, she said, to report child abuse to the police. "I mean, what are you supposed to do with that kind of attitude?" the mother said. She was appalled and exasperated, even though vaguely aware that both feelings were misplaced. Schools have begun educating children about how to get help if they're being beaten or sexually assaulted because they have to. The high incidence of such abuse demands it. But many mothers and fathers have told me that, good intentions aside, this sort of education has amounted to anarchy at home.

"Parents don't take care of their kids. I know that's a problem," Greathouse said. Then, in the next breath, her voice rising, she added, "But these kids today, they don't know the meaning of the word 'no.'" It was hot out and the stream of cars in need of service was steady. She went outside to jockey some more gas. "They don't want for anything, and it's still not enough," elaborated her partner Bund. "It's just really stressful. Go buy a pair of shoes for a three-year-old and you're gonna spend fifteen, maybe twenty bucks. I don't know what [Pam] thinks, but for me, it depresses you and puts you on edge. For a man, there's so much pride and ego involved. It causes divorces."

We can blame television, magazines, Madison Avenue and the images advertisers push. We can blame sexism, the objectification and subjugation of women. Or capitalism, the system's orientation toward consumption. But the truth is that the marketers can manipulate citizens only to the degree that we succumb.

Take for example the way we lap up *Melrose Place* or *Beverly Hills 90210* and such up-scale glitz, then buy heaps of shoddily-made cookie-cut dreck made by companies who are apparently right when they guess that no one will demand they produce anything much better. Take a look at the buttons on clothing these days. Plastic, and about ready to fall off. Skirts and pants are rarely lined. Not to be a total crank, but the nuns who taught me in grammar school would have said that this sloppiness indicated a lack of pride. When did quality clothes made of real fabrics become the province of outrageously priced specialty boutiques? Could it be that the fashion execs in New York presume the vast unwashed masses in America's south or midwest don't know any better or care? And could it be that they've been right? Most of us aren't good consumers. We aren't vigilant enough in forcing the nation's corporations and manufacturers to be responsible and respectful. If we're not conscientious, why should they be? Being a good consumer doesn't mean becoming a full-time grump or committing to a relentless Ralph Naderesque crusade. It simply means being aware of what you're buying, where it comes from and how it's made, reflecting a bit on whether it's environmentally sound, whether it's something you truly need and, perhaps most important, being ready to write a letter or pick up the phone to lodge a complaint when a product is shoddy. It means refusing to be duped, resisting the pressure to buy every "new" or "improved" thing. It means not caring what the Joneses buy and teaching your kids that it's who *wears* the sneakers, not who makes them that matters. It means truly knowing that self-worth isn't purchased at the mall. Rich or poor, male or female, married or single, it's simply a question of claiming—demanding—a place in our market-driven system. Much like democracy, our economy is subject to the pressures brought to bear by people. Whether we're talking about government or business, it is up to us to hold the big players accountable. If not the people, then who?

This stuff is part of everyday life, neither something that need be an obsession nor a task to be left for somebody else. Like our farming forebears who found exercise and fitness were part of everyday life's demands, we must develop and integrate a discipline for the consumer age. Don't say you hate the way the media exploit, then tune in for not one but all three Amy Fisher-Joey Buttafuoco movies. Don't complain that you have no time for reading, then spend what time you do have perusing personality magazines and gossip-driven tabloids. Don't gripe about political corruption, then put off writing a letter to your congressman or supporting a worthy candidate. Don't stand on the escalator when you can walk. Don't throw away what you can recycle. Don't accept 'no' just because everyone else does. Just say "no" to mediocrity, whether it's dished out by Madison Avenue merchants or by the family next door.

And beyond saying no, don't just slink off. Don't just withdraw. Do something. Anything.

Or, as they say, get out of the way.

• • •

The morning I joined them, a guy named Stubby started things off: "America's a mess," he said. And quickly the rest of the gang joined in. Just look at the headlines. Haven't you seen *Geraldo* or *Oprah* lately? What about Washington? Useless. The media? Out of touch. The economy? Sour. The social fabric? Hopelessly frayed. Kids don't have values today. Parents don't care for their kids. I'm not to blame, but someone is. Not you or me, maybe. But someone.

It was about 9 A.M. in Paducah, Kentucky, and I'd happened on a group of roundtable regulars at the Little Castle, Roy Trimble's place. While they were at work assessing the world, the smells of biscuits and gravy, which Roy had been prepping since 3:30 A.M., wafted off the griddle like a whiff of home. Outside, the parking lot was jammed with police cruisers, pickups and assorted American cars. A waitress quickly came over with coffee when Dick McNeil arrived. Soon he'd caught up with the talk, offering a little theory of his own. He called it "coming of age."

The older roundtable regulars rolled their eyes.

"I'm thirty-nine and people my age and younger are maturing," he began, ignoring his critics. "We're becoming citizens. What happened in the 'I want it all for me and the hell with you' years when we were younger can't work in America today. We're growing up. The question people have started asking is: 'Are we going to take the bull by the horns or not? Are we going to turn things around, or sit and watch the country die?'"

Pick up the Formica table at Roy's diner and drop it just about anyplace in America: Conversations like this go on everywhere, all the time. But they are isolated voices, separate pieces of an enormous quilt woven of frustration and despair. In each of these small squares, though, there lies something else. It's true, people tell me they've had it up to here with all the horror to be seen on the 11 o'clock news, and many say they can no longer do much but join the cynicism and apathy that election years bring. But for all the negativism and anxiety, for all the bluster, I have still seen in most all of the Americans I've met an ingredient more potent than all the rest. I've seen it in their eyes and their eagerness to talk issues. I see that they care. Wittingly or not, and regardless of the unfolding of his political career, Ross Perot's presidential run tapped into this energy by offering a point of entry to hundreds of thousands of citizens who had felt locked out by a system at once too small to embrace them and too big to hold.

"[Perot] touched something," said McNeil, by now on his second cup of coffee. "You're seeing a renewed interest, a commitment among people to address problems in their area. And I think it's a feeling out across the country. But the state and federal governments are not in tune. At every turn there's something saying 'no.' You've got to ignore the institutions. And I think people are ready to do that."

Getting a Life 45

Dick McNeil, second from right, gathers with other regulars at the Little Castle in Paducah, Kentucky.

I'd been wandering backroads fairly aimlessly for about a week when I happened by Roy's place. It looked pretty much like the kind of family-run joint I tend to favor: unpretentious, friendly and laid back. They are the places where people go for conversation, to read the newspaper, to hatch big plans or simply pass time. They are where regulars gather to gossip and meals still come made-to-order. Everyone loves them, and yet they are ever harder to find, because we say we love them, then drive up to the nearest take-out window. In a way, this is what we've done as a nation. We love charm, take pride in American quality and style, believe in the importance of character. And yet, we take the drive-thru, like teenagers, loath to delay gratification. It may be shopping at superstores while the old commercial district in the center of town slowly dies. It may be guiltily coughing up a little something for the annual holiday food drive, then standing aloof while the pantry shelves gradually empty through the rest of the year. It may be the teacher you never thanked or the person of a different color that you never took time to know. It may be one more easy shortcut that doesn't lead to dreams or lead the way.

Some months after my first visit, I returned to Paducah to examine a sad case, a crime that had shocked a small city whose residents had imagined themselves exempt from big-city violence. Dick McNeil had called me in New York with a heads-up. "You ought to come down and have a look," he urged. "This is the kind of thing hurting America." What had happened was a random murder, but it was more involved than that. A white high school student on his way home from an after-school restaurant job had been carjacked by five black teenagers, one of whom had fired the fatal shot. Citizens of all colors were shaken and angry. It was not so much a story about urban violence versus rural, black versus white, here versus anyplace else. It was about a moral vacuum that in many ways belonged to us all.

The accused said they'd gone out in search of trouble after watching the video of *Menace II Society*, a hyper-realistic film about the lives and crimes committed by a group of young black men in South-Central Los Angeles. But the murder they were now charged with was about more than Hollywood-inspired hijinks. It was about stupidity and aimlessness and a total lack of regard for human life. "What you have are kids who are raised with no values, no skills, who think the best they can do is make $4 an hour at McDonald's ... no hope of having a family or home, no shot at what we think of as the dream of American life," said Tim Kaltenbach, the state's attorney who was prosecuting the case. On his office wall, like a framed relic of more idealistic times, was a black-and-white photo of John F. Kennedy.

It clearly pained Kaltenbach to try cases like this one, yet another example of degradation beyond anything he'd expected to find in public service. I shared his lament about the loss of morality and purpose among the young. Then I headed a few blocks across town to find Herman and Rhonda Smith, whose son Calvin was among the boys charged in the crime. Though not more than a few minutes' walk from Roy Trimble's friendly diner, it might as well have been a million miles away. The Smith's front porch looked as if it had been bombed, the front steps crumbling and the screen door askew. The bell didn't work and through a window I could see that the living room was dark. I yelled hello and was invited in.

I expected excuses, or oblivion. I found something different: two working parents married nineteen years who had struggled to do right by their three young sons. Herman had plans to fix up the house, which he'd purchased with a down payment saved from his factory foreman's wages. They'd put meals on the table and encouraged their children to study, stay safe, steer clear of trouble. When Calvin became rebellious, the Smiths went to the police. They'd asked that their son be arrested for delinquency. They'd begged social workers to admit him for psychiatric evaluation but were told that their son had to be suicidal. "I told Calvin, 'If you keep hangin' out with these boys, one day they're gonna get you into a world of trouble,'" Smith recalled, his eyes rimmed with tears or fatigue, maybe both.

That day now had arrived. Calvin was in jail and, even with a plea agreement, was looking at a very long sentence. "I tried from February til last Friday just to get him to get a haircut and finally he did," Herman Smith said. "I guess I shoulda done what I was thinking—take him to my hometown. Owensboro. I guess I shoulda got him far away from those boys. But I thought he should be with his father."

This was a father who worked, who cared, who preached basic values. But the rest was not there. "You raise a family—you try—but no one cares. No one cares about your family 'less you do somethin' wrong," the father said, tears rising in his eyes. "I've talked to graduates of the high school—I'm tellin' you *graduates*—who can't tell time. You pretty much have to draw 'em a picture to make 'em understand anything.... They think the only thing there is, is to be is a basketball star. They don't see anything else. I tried to tell Calvin there was something else, but the world out there, that world is a lot bigger than me."

Smith gave me directions to a nearby house where Calvin's girlfriend lived. She was a teenager whose name, like the boy's mother's, was Rhonda. "I knew when he was hangin' out with them he was headed toward trouble because they was always in trouble," Rhonda Johnson said of the boys caught up in the carjacking and murder. In addition to Calvin, the father of her soon-to-be-born baby, she also had a cousin and several friends who were involved. Clearly a little flattered that a reporter was stopping by, she waved me into her family's living room. It was dark, the faux-wood paneling buckling under the airless heat. She was flippant, her slightly older sister Regina doing most of the talking at first. Their mother was at work, they said. "People's always askin' me about [the murder] now, you know, because I was Calvin's girlfriend. They throw it up in my face, being all nosy. What's gonna happen to Calvin? What's happenin' with

Calvin? Well, *I don't know* what's happenin' with Calvin," Rhonda finally said. "He always be saying he wants to get married. He be calling me from jail all the time now, cryin' and goin' on. But I don't know. He says if he could get a second chance he would change, go to church and get a job, change his life around. But I don't know. 'Change his life around.' What's that really mean?"

And truly, she seemed at a loss. The interview was falling flat when a band of sullen teenage boys in bandannas and baggy shorts sauntered into the room, a few toddlers trailing behind. The room grew very quiet. I stiffened. To break the tension I introduced myself. More silence ensued. I explained the reason for my visit. Still, more silence. It was growing pretty uncomfortable, my thighs squeaking as I shifted on the plastic-covered sofa. "I don't get it," I said, trying another tack. "Lots of people like me don't get it. Translate. Try explaining how Calvin and the others landed in jail."

Jessie Johnson looked at me a good thirty seconds. He looked like he couldn't be bothered. We sat in more silence until at last he said: "My life is gone."

This kid . . . well he wasn't a kid. He was a twenty-year-old man with an infant daughter and too many friends dead or locked up in jail. Those on the outside, he said, not excluding himself, were just marking time, "hanging out because you aren't going to be anything anyway." Jessie had had something approximating a public school education but, he said, "I got no more life. My life's about being depressed and being too small to play football or basketball. I wanted to make it big in football, but they said I'd never make it so I dropped out."

"You can't help but be depressed when you see so much—the things people say and do," said his sister Rhonda, suddenly coming to life. Her eyes now seemed to have somebody behind them, somebody with something to say. "It's not just what we see, but what we've seen," continued Jessie. "Me, Calvin, Steven, we used to play baseball. We been knowing each other since we were kids. We all be hanging out together, but we knew. We knew we weren't going anywhere."

I had nothing to offer. Here around me were a bunch of kids, ages two to twenty, a couple of the younger ones now squalling, the older ones quietly angry. All of them seemed lost, yet none of them far out of reach. I sat with them for a long while that afternoon, eventually putting aside my notebook. Lamely I tried to offer some advice. But it was useless. They could see no alternatives. They saw no job opportunities, no life beyond the run-down blocks that had been their only home. So their friends and cousins were now facing life in jail. So what? They never expected a whole lot different.

"You want to make something, but there's no way. There's no one out there to talk to me. There's programs, but I don't know what that's about. I just know I'm alone. All I got is my family. This I take to my heart. I'd rather die than see someone run over my sisters or brothers," Jessie said, now up and pacing around the room. "I want to take care. But I feel like . . . I don't know. We're out here on our own. There's nothing for me."

These weren't stupid kids. We were clustered together in a dark room, and Jessie had scared me a little at first, but I wasn't scared anymore. Not of him, anyway. I was scared by the vacuum, by the futures abandoned before the littlest ones in the group had even learned to walk. Before me was America's nightmare, a bunch of kids with no sense of purpose, no connection with possibility. I thought again of the short distance between these shadowy homes and the heart of downtown, where I'd first happened by Roy Trimble's for breakfast so many months before. Though only a few blocks away from Rhonda and Jessie Johnson's house, from Rhonda, Herman and Calvin Smith's rickety front porch, the expanse between their lives and the well-tended front gardens in the "better" part of town seemed too broad to broach.

"You're lookin' at it," Jessie said as I got back in my rental car. "This is America."

I forced myself to look in the rearview mirror, but my foot was firmly on the gas pedal as I sped away.

"A lot of people saw us in the newspaper," Roy Trimble told me a little later that day when I stopped by his place for some lunch. The piece I'd written about his diner had been published nationally a few months before, a front-page newspaper clipping was now framed and hanging behind the cash register near the front door. "People called from all around the country to talk about that article you wrote. It was kind of fun, like a little shot in the arm for a little place like this," he said. But the restaurant business was tough as ever. And it looked unlikely that Trimble's kids would take over when he was ready to retire some years down the road. Trimble said he'd been wondering whether he'd stick it out that long. "You know, I carry a gun with me to work in the early morning. It's dark out. You don't know what could happen. The world's just gone crazy. That's all," he said. "You've got kids shooting kids even in a small town like this one. And what do we do? What do we do? My wife and I took a walk around our neighborhood the other night and passed three sets of people. Three sets of people, and two didn't stop to say 'Hi.' And that's [here] in the country. You really do wonder what kind of a country we're becoming."

I wondered for a long time about Jessie Johnson and

what he might become. I told him when we met that there was a lot out there for him, that it was just a matter of finding the way. It wasn't an outright lie, but it felt disingenuous nonetheless. A bumper-sticker message wasn't going to undo all the others, erase all the messages he'd rightly or wrongly perceived as being all about "no." He was a young black man with a baby and wife, no skills and little regard for whatever analysis ideologues or pundits or social engineers might offer. He was depressed. He had lost too many friends to drugs, to crime, to hopelessness.

Recently I found out what happened to Jessie. He's at Green River State Prison, along with Herman Smith's son, Calvin. A string of cigarette burns and bruises told the story. He pleaded guilty to the abuse of his daughter.

These were kids who, in theory, could have chosen something different. But whether they couldn't or wouldn't, it doesn't seem to make much of a difference. If they remain stuck in perpetual adolescence, the result is the same. And we all pay the price.

Getting a Grip
Facing the Demons
3

"That's truly disgusting," a friend said, and no one at the table disagreed. I'd just confessed a dirty secret: I'd still not gotten over "the Whopper thing." My latest breakdown had occurred only a few weeks before while I was out reporting a sad story I really didn't want to tell. I'd tried to beg off, but had no compelling excuse to offer my editors. I'd just had other plans, other things on my personal agenda. So, frustrated and a little lost out on the road, I broke down like a big baby and sought solace in an old standby quick fix.

An hour after my plane had touched down, there it was beside me: my unholy mix. On the rental car's passenger seat lay a pack of strong cigarettes, a bottle of soda and a big ol' box of Whoppers. You know, the malted milk balls that come in a milk carton. I don't even like them, the way they grate like chalk against your teeth. I guess I was just glad for the company. At some point some years ago, these things had become my trusty travel companions, a sort of irrational care package for the road. They're unhealthy and do nothing to comfort me after the first flash of guilty pleasure has passed. Inevitably, at the end of these trips, I gather up the remnants—the crumpled cigarette pack, half-eaten box of candy, bottles rolling around on the car floor—and toss the whole lot into a trash bin at the airport, swearing not to behave so badly again. Inevitably, though, for all my resolutions, I'm likely as not to skulk off to the nearest K-mart the next time some assignment sends me out on the road again.

I've still not quite figured out what it is. Partly, I think, it's just kind of a naughty kick. Partly, it's a little device that gets me through the "hunt and forage" mode that goes with driving into a strange town, a reliable anchor and ally, an easy ritual on disorienting trips made without advance reservations. Maybe it eases the anxiety, helps me gloss over the doubts about whether this story will be the one I don't come home with, the piece I can't nail down, the trip on which the blank computer screen will blink back at me, stay blank forever.

The point is that it's a lazy device and one that long ago stopped working in any real sense. And yet, I keep doing it, like a sad little Pavlovian dog.

Back over dinner in New York, soon after I'd made my little confession, the conversation moved on, turning to topics in the headlines. We all have these conversations fairly regularly, the ones about health care, jobs, education, youth, crime, drugs. In short, the future of our communities and country at large. And mostly they end when the bottle of wine runs out or the phone rings or the barbecue coals are reduced to smoldering ash. Everyone agrees that the nation is facing serious problems, and then guiltily we return to our naughty, comfortable little patterns. Occasionally someone will vow to do more, to volunteer or go out and buy a highly recommended book. Mostly, though, these conversations just kind of sputter out, wind to a fruitless end.

"The problems are so overwhelming."

"I'm so busy. I just don't have the time."

"Hey, I pay taxes and support my family. That's more than a lot of people do today."

"Things are out of control. Sure. But what can I really do?"

Pick one. They are excuses all of us have used from time to time. And all of them are valid to one degree or another. But that's not quite enough. Like the noxious brew I reflexively buy for myself when the going gets tough, these mechanisms may have evolved for a reason and they may even help. But it's in the short term, and we know it. We all know it as surely as I know the standard stomach ache that inevitably accompanies my ugly malted milk ball-tobacco-soda pop mix. "How many times do I have to learn?" I ask myself contemptuously. How many times, indeed.

How many times do any of us have to learn? Knowing what's good for us is allegedly what separates parents from children. Doing what's right even when it requires a little restraint or a new sort of understanding is what marks the difference between mature adults and self-absorbed adolescents. Breaking old patterns, defying formulas that do not work, are measures of growth. Sometimes they make the difference between slow death and bracing strides.

On my refrigerator there is a little clipping that has moved with me now through seven years and apartments in nearly as many cities. It tells a little parable, one version or another of which many people have heard. The one I came across was a *Reader's Digest* excerpt from a book called *Winning by Letting Go*:

"In India, people have caught monkeys by setting out a small box with a tasty nut in it. There is an opening in the box large enough for the monkey to thrust in his hand, but too small for him to withdraw it once he's clutched the nut. When the monkey has grabbed the prize, he must either let go and regain his freedom or keep hold and stay trapped.

"Most monkeys hold onto the nut, making it easy for hunters to pick them up. People have been known to get caught in the same kind of trap. The person who puts the goodie in the box controls the person who grabs it, but if we are willing to let go of the goodies, we are free of control."

Who hasn't held on too long, fought wildly to resuscitate a terminal relationship or dead-end job, clung jealously to a childhood wound or adult disappointment? Taken to an extreme, we have held on and held on to the "goodies" that American life promises even as they've begun to shrivel away within our grasp. The thing is, though, we are the keepers in many ways of our own traps. This is true of educated, privileged people who never seem to have enough. And it is likewise true of undereducated, underprivileged people who claim there is no place to start.

But it's more than a question of control or self-possession, though those are important tools to feeling a sense of place in our communities and homes. It's also a question of responsibility. We can make excuses and continually feel slightly sick to our stomachs, or we can actually stand up, get a grip, move forward together as grown-up adults.

• • •

The parking lot out back of the Quality Inn in Greencastle, Pennsylvania, was jammed with well-waxed Camaros on the winter evening I pulled off Interstate 81 in search of some dinner and a good night's rest. I figured the motel was a hub for Kiwanis or bingo. Maybe the bar had a lively happy hour. But I had it wrong. The young people who had driven from miles around to this squat brick building had come to work out at an adjoining health club. Inside, men in sweatpants and Stanley Kowalski-style sleeveless T-shirts with weightlifters belts draped themselves here and there over free-weight racks, warming up and saying hi with high-fives. In a room lined with mirrors, about two dozen women in leotards and tans purchased at a nearby mall stared at themselves, crunching their rear ends to the relentless beat of a cross-over rap song.

"That's the state of the world today," chanted pop star Janet Jackson. "And uh-one and uh-two and three and four," chanted the aerobics teacher. "That's the state of the world today," came the lyrics, again and again.

I was mesmerized. All these young people, so much energy focused so keenly on the loud music and mirrors. "It makes you feel better about yourself," said Sheryl Unger, who had resolved to take a few inches off her hips and thighs after hitting her thirtieth birthday. This night she was doing back-to-back aerobics classes. "It's made me a lot happier. I mean, it's what most of us want, right? A perfect man and a perfect bod."

She laughed. Her eyes were rueful. We were in the locker room by now, balanced on the edge of a tired-looking Jacuzzi. Unger had little patience with pondering America's preoccupation with fitness and beauty. My leading questions about whether her time might be more altruistically spent elsewhere met with no reply. Keeping her weight down and her recent relationship together was about all she could handle outside of her job as an office assistant. She didn't seem to care much about politics or crime or global issues. Maybe in part because she planned no children. "I don't know. The things that you see in the world growing up reflect how you feel about yourself,"

Unger said, her gaze softening. "I'm a very insecure person. A woman with no teeth could be standing next to me and I'd say she looks better.... The boyfriends I've always had in the past were abusers, but I felt 'I've got to stay here and take it. This is the way life is.'"

Unger said she didn't feel that way anymore. Or, more precisely, she was doing her best to stave off those feelings of self-doubt and impotence with physical discipline. Sometimes it worked. Sometimes it didn't. "But at least you feel like you're doing something for yourself," she said. "Even if you're not, you feel like you are. It's all psychological, I guess, in the end. You're taking control of yourself, and that's the first step to self-help."

We're talking here about the self-esteem thing. And it's a tempting target, what with Gloria Steinem having written a best-seller about it and Garry Trudeau having lampooned it in his "Doonesbury" comic strip. In California, a whole commission was created to cultivate it and psychotherapists in pseudo-Chanel suits have referred to it so regularly on afternoon chat shows that audience members and panelists now beat them to the punch by diagnosing themselves. It seems almost any behavior or misbehavior, from addiction to violence to bad parenting to juvenile delinquency, may be heaped under the rubric of low self-esteem. More and more people have turned to self-help groups or counselors to combat the scourge. I've heard a lot people talk about how they are "working on themselves," almost as if they are broken-down cars or houses in need of repair. This isn't necessarily entirely indulgent, for surely it's hard to do right by others when in a state of psychic breakdown. The problem is, feeling good isn't just about... well, feeling good. It's also about feeling bad, accepting blame and making sacrifices. It's about reaching beyond self-absorption into the lives of others.

As a nation we do this well when confronting a crisis, but what of the everyday? How often do we retreat to the mirror, obsess on what we're not and all the things we might do if only . . . "If only I could lose ten pounds, get rid of a few inches here and here," Unger said, surveying herself with a laugh. "I know it won't make my life perfect, but it'll make it better. It will, won't it? That's what the commercials and magazines tell you."

How amused our pioneering ancestors would be at our obsession with fitness. Surely they couldn't have imagined a nation of couch potatoes with sugar-laden Big Gulps in one hand and a bag of chips in the other. They did not sit for hours, channel surfing the boob tube. They did not have glossy images plastered everywhere with the subtext, "This is success." We have developed an entire culture and industry around fitness, something that was at one time a natural part of the rhythm of life. You worked in a field instead of an office. You walked or rode your bicycle to the market instead of sliding up in a car. You chased after children instead of setting them up with a videotape. You took a long stroll at night and visited with neighbors instead of flopping down beside the air-conditioner while sweaty life continued somewhere outdoors.

We are not, of course, going to return to an era featuring the mule-drawn plow. Still, it's interesting to look at how we waste time and gas making a dozen loops around the shopping mall parking lot in search of the closest possible slot, then rush through errands to get down to the health club for a workout.

For all our gyrations, I recently read of a Harris Poll that had found 69 percent of Americans were overweight as compared with 58 percent in 1983. It's almost as if we refuse to take anything but the long way around to the things closest to our hearts. Certainly being in good shape, doing all the basic stuff doctors long have urged, makes a tremendous difference. But, come on. We all know that in the end weight is not the determining factor for happiness or the stuff of true self-esteem.

First, before all else, you have to have a true pulse. Without a sense of purpose, a passion for participation and possibility, some sense of connection with other people, not much else truly counts. Perfection—physical or otherwise—may seem the goal, but ultimately it cannot deliver the nourishment we desperately craved.

"I've been up there with the best of them," cracked Rachelle Burk, an outspoken young New Jersey woman I met on an airplane a few years ago. "When I was single, I tried every diet there was: Weight Watchers, the Diet Center, the Cambridge diet, the F-Plan diet, the Scarsdale diet.... It was pretty much encompassing because I was miserable. I look back at my diaries and see how totally miserable I was being fat and boyfriendless," said the thirty-five-year-old social worker who eventually met her husband, the father of her two children, through a personal ad. "Like a lot of people, I wanted a quick fix. I just wanted to feel better so badly. A therapist told me a few years ago, in talking about the history of my weight problem—addictions really of any kind—that it started when my mother died. I gained weight when I lost love and lost it when I found love with Simon. With Simon, I was unconditionally loved. I was safe when not a lot feels safe in this world."

Slowly, the excess weight slipped away as a new world opened up to Rachelle. The tears and loneliness eased, "the isolation I always felt between me and the rest of the world finally ended," she said recently. "I wasn't ever even looking for perfection. I just wanted normalcy. I just wanted a sense of belonging, of being in the flow of life.

And when that happened, the compulsion just left me. There wasn't this need to fill my emptiness with food anymore."

Rachelle Burk would never bill herself as a sage. And yet, after many unhappy years of obesity, she'd hit on something more basic that any calorie count, more filling than food, more sustaining than any job, course of exercise or psychotherapy could ever be. She'd found a life, new ways to care and a strong sense that others cared back. She'd found roots, and over the last decade they'd only grown stronger. "I've kept the weight stable. I've got a family, four jobs, friends, community connections. And that comes from not feeling alone. It's why I'm a great supporter of support groups like OA (Overeaters Anonymous). They relieve that isolation," she said. "And when that isolation—all the fear—reduces, entire lives can change."

• • •

Every time I've gotten into a rental car, whether in New Hampshire or Iowa or France, I've thought to myself: Maybe this trip I'll find it. Maybe this time something will descend to say: "Ah yes, at last you are home." In my fantasy, I drive up to a thriving main square, something by Coltrane spinning on the local jazz station. A Cary Grant revival is up on Main Street's marquee and nearby a river is running, swift and clean. The living in my town would be inexpensive and an open-air green market well-trafficked each week, a community college performance of Mozart's Requiem would be in rehearsal and a bakery's window filled with fresh bread, still warm. There would be a quirky little house that needed fixing up, a place with a fireplace, space for a garden. Here, maybe, I would at last find something like peace. Work would not be a worry, for there would be a lively local newspaper with an available job, and neighbors would look out for each other, and me, since I now would be one of them. So it's a fantastic ideal, so friends laugh when I share it from time to time. They joke about coming to scrape me up off a termite-eaten back porch, prying me from a bottle of whiskey as I murmur something about surrendering to glorious rural charm. They may be right, dismissing my talk of packing up for West Virginia or Tennessee. I drove many miles while looking for my version of the American dream.

Crossroads, Louisiana, seemed an apt name when I plucked it off the map. An editor had asked me to get some "country-type" reaction to the Democratic convention and Bill Clinton as he accepted his party's nomination. It was a last-minute assignment, and I took off on a dime. What I remember most is missing my Shreveport connection because, in a rush, I hopped on an Atlanta airport subway going in the wrong direction. The mishaps continued from there: I jogged breathlessly up to the rental car counter at my final destination only to find no one around; tore off on the highway only to speed miles to the west when I meant to be southbound. Pulling off to check my map at a rest stop, I found myself awkwardly among young male prostitutes doing business with truckdrivers and traveling salesmen probably well known around their hometowns. I was lost, and growing a bit frantic as my deadline approached.

I stopped at several small towns before straggling into Dixie Inn, where Bud's liquor store was doing brisk business and Bill Clinton's acceptance speech, the one I was supposed to be covering, was about to begin. An hour later he would step up to a podium and speak of the "new covenant" he hoped everyone would share. I asked the proprietors at Bud's if they knew a good citizen, someone who would let me sit in their home during the speech. It is bizarre to think back now on myself, blindly dialing the phone. "Call Ms. Lee," the folks at Bud's Liquor had said. "She's someone who cares."

She was a bit taken aback at first, but soon agreed to let me come over. And so I came to sit with Ms. Lee, a schoolteacher, as Bill Clinton delivered his speech. The government has lost touch, he told his nationwide audience from a platform in New York. People are crying out for change, "pleading for it," he said, "but government is in the way." Echoing John F. Kennedy, he challenged Americans to join in building a future based not on what we could take, but on what we could give. Madison Square Garden was alive with cheers. Bud's was selling booze at a steady pace. Earlier a young man had dismissed me: "What's the point of even listening?" he said, hoisting a six-pack. "There's nothing to hear."

But Jerri Lee was listening, balancing her baby grandson on one knee. She was fed up, too, but far from defeated. "If you want a piece of the American pie, you have to fight tooth and nail," she said. "The people must participate—the people—*all of the people*. We've got to support each other again if we're going to have the democratic society we boast about." Oh dear, she said, "Don't get Ms. Lee going."

As an educator, black woman, parent and active citizen, she had her fingers in a lot of pies, from working for her teachers union to serving on a local task force on race relations. She'd raised three children while teaching high school over a quarter of a century. She worshipped on Sundays, kept up on current events, cared deeply about what was going on in her community. "I've been blessed. I am a product of a very fine, hard-working Christian home," said Ms. Lee, forty-eight. "My mother was a homemaker and Daddy was always working. All nine kids graduated college. We understood the meaning of family. We found contentment in trying to make a difference. Not in great ways—just by caring."

Today, she said, this attitude seemed sadly rare. Waving toward the television, where Democrats in funny hats cheered on, she lamented that "so many people feel they have nothing to do with any of this."

It was getting late and Ms. Lee had things to do around the house. I left her as she headed out back to fire up her smokehouse. She was having a small get-together the following day. It was time I found someplace to write my story, a story I knew would be hopelessly skewed. Too many voices, too many leaps. "Go right across the tracks to Pine and take another right. You'll find your way back to town," and with that my brief acquaintance with Ms. Lee came to an end.

Dixie Inn reminded me of so many other towns, liquor stores and gas station mini-marts at their abandoned hearts. A ways down the state road you come upon the fast-food landscape, a string of familiar brand names. In this instance, late at night with an unwritten story yet to file, Taco Bell was a welcome sight. Teenagers lolled in the parking lot. More voices; more leaps. "What's the use of me voting? My vote ain't gonna do me no better or worse," said a guy of about eighteen, who had not been the least interested in hearing any candidate's acceptance speech. I got a burrito to go. Though I usually prefer independent motels, this night I just wanted a trusty chain with a good working phone. I wound up in a place that stands out in my memory because it was perhaps the single most depressing room I've ever stayed in. There was no toilet paper, no soap or window to raise. Actually, there once had been windows but for reasons unclear the owners had sealed them with slabs of sheet metal. I didn't want to touch anything. The parking lot was congested with huge, jacked-up trucks whose oversized-floodlights I've never quite understood. By now it was after midnight and there I sat with my Taco Bell dinner and computer propped up on a chair, struggling to sum up rural America's reaction to what was then for Bill Clinton only a presidential dream. Instead, I kept wondering about all those trucks outside in the darkened parking lot. I guessed at rates of pregnancy, poverty, crime and violent death. I thought about unemployment, illiteracy and all the other indicators that consistently ranked Louisiana near the bottom on the national map. I pondered whether this ring of no-tell rooms was occupied by adulterous lovers or teenagers soon to be parents. How many could really afford the $30 occupancy rate? Were a few hours in one of these stale rooms worth the price? Who were these people? While Jerri Lee dozed in her tidy brick home just up the road, I spent the night fully dressed and fitful, eventually slipping into Bette Davis's *Dark Passage*, watching a TV suspended on a metal arm over my rumpled bed.

I felt miserably alone. What was the point? At about 5 A.M., one by one, the trucks began to leave.

I'd talked in such a brief time with so many people who felt helpless or scared, like teenagers stunned by pubescence's first disorienting hormonal blows. The bursts of anger and confusion seemed so unremitting that they'd stopped all growth. People had told me they felt shaken, desperately cut off. For many, a kind of paralysis had set in. "We're in a world of hurt," Donnie Perkins, a father and laborer, had told me early in the evening, when I'd stopped for directions at a roadside shack known locally as The Pines.

To be sure, there are many who, like Jerri Lee, Donnie Perkins and his wife, choose to vote, organize, reach out to neighbors, family and friends. They are the ones who, despite the loneliness and disconnection, without headlines or the political attention, are still fighting on.

But I kept hearing Donnie Perkins. "We're in a world of hurt down here," he said. "And a lot of times it just seems like no one understands." Like me in my rental car, forever in search of an ideal home, so many Americans are profoundly threatened by the future, desperately unsure of everything except this certainty: You've got to drive on.

• • •

Patrons at Merv Griffin's riverboat casino were lined up along the bar like shorebirds, their backs shadowed against a bank of windows beyond which the Ohio River ran flat and silver under the afternoon sun. "What can I get for you?" the barkeep asked Rich Richeson. It was such a nice question. Familiar and easy to answer. Rich Richeson wanted a beer, and in seconds a beer was before him. He wanted a cigarette, and so he lighted one up. Simple. So wonderfully achievable. "Not a lot left that's so easy," Richeson said, then said no more. The crowd was genial but muted, even contemplative. No one had yet drunk too much or lost too big at the gaming tables. No one was particularly bleak or overly gay. A sort of soothing anonymity suffused the place while everyone waited, shoulder to shoulder, for the riverboat to come in. And when it did, they boarded together, hoping for a lucky streak or at least a little camaraderie. Of course, the downside was obvious. Of course, gambling can be dangerously addictive, a stupid waste of time and money. But it all felt so good. How lovely to nurse a drink and jackpot dreams.

It's probably not entirely coincidental that in the midst of diminished expectations state lotteries have cropped up around the nation while casinos like Merv Griffin's have flourished in small towns like Metropolis, Illinois, whose other claim to fame is being Superman's home. On Indian reservations around the map and along the banks of cash-strapped cities like East St. Louis and New Orleans, gambling carries a powerful allure: a shot at quick money and a little escape. Even though the odds are heavily stacked, you can go to the table and at least find hope, or the illusion of it. Say hello to the one-armed bandit. You never know.

"I guess everybody thought we was going to have things given to us on a silver platter," said Richeson, a thirty-three-year-old construction worker who looked both young and old. "It feels like the party kept getting bigger and bigger. And then—like that—it ended. All of a sudden, things started to shrink." This was not how life was supposed to go. "I expected pretty much what people around my age expected: A nice life. No sweat." And it was looking good, too. Out of high school, contractors threw steady work his way. The pay was decent and the pace none too taxing. He had money for shiny new cars, as many cable channels as the market could offer, upscale vacations and nights on the town. He got married and a little later had a son. Then life took a bum turn. Richeson was laid off. In 1989, he bought his first used car. "Things aren't any better now than four or five years ago. Maybe a little. But basically the outlook isn't too good," he said, saying no more. A few minutes went by in silence, until finally Richeson looked up from his beer and, his voice lifting a little, offered, "Things haven't changed, but I guess what we're learning is how to adapt."

Something *had* changed. Maturity had begun to stir.

Learning to adapt had been about learning something more. It had been about understanding that some of the old rules were better, that having it all wasn't necessarily the best. The used car, Richeson discovered, ran just fine. The fixer-upper house he and his wife bought instead of the spanky new one they'd envisioned had a certain charm at half the price. Buying generic cigarettes and using coupons at the grocery and cutting down on cable had added up to a family vacation. "It wasn't anything fancy, but it was real nice."

Running through this list, reassessing what had become of his life, Richeson perked up a little. It wasn't half bad.

"When I was growing up, we had three channels on TV and it was enough," he said. "It feels like you're going backwards and it's hard. But maybe we're just growing up, learning when enough is enough. Maybe, like they say, more in some ways is less."

• • •

"I'm an addict, and I shouldn't be. It's not what I was brought up to be," said Diane Black, a lovely, if troubled blonde perched on a bench beside the San Francisco Bay. She'd been peering out over the shimmering water for some time, deep in thought. Dressed neatly in a skirt, her hair swept back in a conservative headband, I'd pegged her for a real estate agent or perhaps the owner of one of Sausalito's trendy tourist boutiques. She had the look of a young mother, or maybe a newly engaged bride-to-be. Her fiancé might have driven any of the BMWs or Mercedes that kept passing by.

In fact, it turned out, she was widowed. Her husband had overdosed several weeks prior, ending his life at thirty-three. "He knew better," she said, emotionless. "My husband and I, we both grew up in nice families. We had good upbringings, advantages. We should have been A-OK. But Americans have a way of being miserable. Especially younger ones."

Ms. Black, thirty-two, had grown up on the cutting edge of a human potential movement that has today spread throughout the culture. In city projects and suburban subdivisions alike, concepts like twelve-step recovery and co-dependence and self-esteem are the coin of the realm. In airports, businessmen and women snag a copy of the latest best-selling tract on managerial prowess or tips for unbelievably hot sex. Millions of people have gravitated toward a narrow Christian right even as a growing number of converted Buddhists and Muslims have followed a spiritual path away from Western tradition.

This, and so much more, suggests a mass yearning for some anchor in a stormy sea.

Looking out across the San Francisco Bay at all the old, familiar childhood landmarks, I understood this urge as surely as I did the urge to roam. While living in Paris during my early twenties, I had the steady sense that I didn't know quite where I was going. I just knew that wherever it was, I was not there. So eventually I bought another one-way plane ticket. This time to the Middle East. It makes me laugh to think now of saying good-bye to my mother, who was on a visit in France. As I was boarding a train on my way to the airport we exchanged a few last, hurried words. Then, as I was climbing aboard, she yelped out from the platform: "Just tell me one thing. Why can't you go to Club Med like everyone else?" She laughed. I laughed, then I cried as the train pulled away. Her question has rung in my ears ever since. On that long ramble, which took me through a half-dozen countries over several months, I pondered my place in life. I could have wandered on forever, hitching one more ride on someone's small boat, crossing another border, climbing another small mountain just to see what lay beyond. But on a mountain in Turkey, everything came to a stop. I confronted the possibility that I'd traveled too far, that the only way forward was to turn determinedly back.

Now here I was some years later, sitting in my hometown's backyard, a national reporter with a cat and a co-op and a steady circle of friends. And yet, no less than Diane Black, I was in many ways running as hard and fast as ever, even as my thirtieth birthday came into view. Over the years, in the course of covering so many disparate stories, I'd yet to find my lead. I'd mostly met people who, like me, had tried and failed and tried again to locate some balance in their lives. Like me, they had taken many baby steps and were only slowly approaching safe places. But bit by bit, I had the sense of the common thread, the common urge to make a place that could truly be called a home. We had come to this not as older generations had, by default, but after long years of searching and at great personal expense.

Maybe for all our experimentation and agitation, for all the high hopes and boundless promises of youth, we have arrived at something closer to the long road that is human, flawed, in need of constant maintenance and repair. Maybe the demands of real life aren't so tough after all. Maybe they offer their own rewards. Maybe the rewards are found most of all in striding forward and standing firm. And maybe there ain't a whole lot more than the journey itself.

Maybe, in the late songwriter Harry Chapin's words, "It's got to be the going, not the getting there that's good."

"I wonder if in the '90s we're not beginning to see a

shift back toward an appreciation of close relationships and a communal mentality. For all our pursuit of individual happiness, there's no evidence that we're happier today than when we had much less," said David Myers, a social psychologist and author of *The Pursuit of Happiness: Who Is Happy—and Why*. "People who are preoccupied with themselves, self-focused, tend not to be as happy as those who are focused on things outside themselves. . . . It's the gap between our expectations and attainments that defines happiness. So if our expectations rise as rapidly as our achievements, then we will never be happy. It's not a sell-out or compromise to simplify our aspirations. It's liberating."

It's liberating, Myers said, to think that life is about committing to things far more basic—and attainable—than some notion of perfect bliss. Maybe Dorothy was onto something. Forget the land of Oz, she resolved at the end of her yellow-brick road. Happiness is found in the gardens we tend, the people we love. It is possible to travel all over the map, psychically and physically, professionally and spiritually. You can buy into the promise of a magic potion or cure-all cream. But the truth is, as any number of teenagers who have bought the newest pimple polish will tell you, things pretty much take their course. The course taken by the most peaceful people seems to have little to do with easy gratification and everything to do with building a committed life bit by imperfect bit.

"I think I'm beginning to get it," Ms. Black said toward the end of our conversation that sunny day. "It's taken a while, like three decades. But I think I've got the message: We're the makers of our own beds. That's it, don't you think? I'm not sure, but I think I'm finally growing up."

I'm not quite sure where Diane Black is today. I followed her for awhile, but she moved around and we soon fell out of touch. I've got no idea of whether she had had luck getting a job, making a new life, staying clean. Wherever she is, I hope she is well. Because she was, in her own way, as much of a grown-up as anyone I've met on the road.

Getting Over It

Moving Forward Means Defying Despair

4

In my neighborhood on Manhattan's Upper West, a community I've been told is one of the most densely populated in the world, residents had carved out something beautiful. From a vacant lot long known as a magnet for drug dealers and rats, people had joined forces more than a dozen years ago and moved in. They'd reclaimed a sorry piece of their neighborhood that had for so long been lost, removing bricks and syringes, picking through discarded bottles and collecting bags full of trash. Slowly, over the years, out of this wasteland a garden grew.

In springtime, it was here that you could spot the first signs of life nudging up through the icy ground. By midsummer, plots tended with enormous love spilled over with beans and tomatoes and collard greens. The friendly paths through this little space were lined with daffodils and roses and tulips. At the center of it all was a huge willow tree—the only one in Manhattan, according to some—whose leaves played in the afternoon breeze, a gentle guard against the overheated city just beyond the gate. If you happened into the garden any time of the day, you were as likely as not to find James Romero, a pint-sized kid who would give you a tour, gravely pointing out each species of plant, the hiding places preferred by stray cats, the gazebo in which mothers gathered with strollers at the peak of the day.

Then one morning, it was gone. In minutes, a bulldozer had eaten it up.

Dispatched by the city, the heavy equipment had arrived around dawn, when perhaps officials thought that the garden's family of supporters would be on their ways to work or still asleep in bed. As their work began, a crowd steadily grew, people standing silently behind baby-blue barricades, their mouths half-open. Some cried. I counted at least a dozen police cars and twice as many edgy police. Perhaps they expected trouble. But it was too late, the picnic table and gazebo had been flattened. The little brick-lined walkways mowed over, the vegetable plots ground under. As they went at the willow tree, people physically drew back, as if one of their own limbs were being slowly, tortuously broken.

"Where will the cats go now?" a little boy asked his father. Looking down, the father could only shake his head.

The city had long fought to clear the garden, which had never belonged to the citizens except by default. It was a narrow parcel wedged between two tired brownstones across from an overcrowded public high school, an orphaned slice of New York about which for years no one seemed particularly to care. At least, not until the housing authority received a federal grant tied to a deadline. Ground had to be broken, or the funds foregone. On the municipal map, The Dome's garden no doubt had looked like available land. The thing was, those who had nurtured it came to own this empty plot. And so when word that the garden was in jeopardy spread, a vigorous campaign was quickly mounted.

Partisans did all the right things. Attorneys volunteered, making pro-bono arguments in court. The Dome's director and staff spoke to news reporters, who wrote sympathetic national stories. And everyone—hundreds of people of all ages, races, economic circumstances—filled the halls where city counselors and local board members met. It was democracy in action and, for a long time, people felt hope.

At one such community board meeting, held in a church basement, children made their pleas. After the petitions for outdoor cafe permits had been granted and noise control grievances had been settled, the focus turned to the garden. The jammed-to-capacity room began to shift. Little James Romero stepped forward to address officials whom the citizens in attendance could choose not to re-elect.

"I've been real depressed lately," he said in his small, serious voice. "My mom and dad are breaking apart. My home, well, there's a lot of confusion there. And stuff. But the garden, I came there and got happy." He paused for a minute, his expression one that belonged on a very old man. "I've been going there three years now. To the garden. If you close this garden," he said, thumping his chest, "you'll break my heart. Hundreds of kids come to play there and mess around. There's no place for us in this city. The garden is a place. That's all I've got to say."

The room went wild. The city officials' faces seemed to indicate that they'd been touched.

"I'm eleven years old and I've been in the garden for three or four years," said a girl who had brought crayon pictures as visual aids. "I want to save the garden because there are animals in there and we built the garden ourselves. In the summer, when there's nothing to do, we can go in the garden and plant flowers and take them to our mothers."

"Maybe you don't need a garden. But we need ours," added another little girl in a squeaky, soft voice. "We really do. It's the truth."

"If we're not careful the garden will be all messed up and I won't like that. No way, Jose," said another little boy in his turn. "I bet I know something none of y'all know: When the man worm and the girl worm get together they both have babies. I learned that in the garden." He blushed. Everyone laughed. "You got that right," shouted out Mildred, one of the garden's older devotees. "You tell 'em, baby!"

The housing authority officials clearly were not amused.

The process ground on, with small victories hard earned. A year or so later, despite more board meetings, more pleas, more media coverage and letters to the mayor, more court appeals and prayer vigils and injunctions, the garden swiftly died. After the bulldozers left, aluminum siding was laid up against the garden fence, obscuring the wreckage. But everyone knew what once had been there, what no longer was

In the days that followed, signs began to appear, lamentations in big block letters, bits of poetry scrawled on scraps of paper, starburst photographs of flowers and foliage taken on sunnier days, wobbly watercolor pictures painted with children's hands.

"You have broken our hearts," read a note written on a piece of napkin. "But we will not die."

• • •

Teenagers specialize in feeling that life isn't fair. And it's no wonder why. Waking up to the big, wide world is a tremendous jolt. Realizing that you're not the center of the universe but, rather, just one of so many players is enormously intimidating. How do you go about making a mark? How do you accomplish all that you hope to in the face of so many newfound limitations? What's really out there, anyway? It isn't fair.

But fair or not, we all wobble out into the world, frequently wary and in constant need of reassurance. As a young nation, we've enjoyed plenty: enormous liberty, wealth and opportunity. In some senses, we've had a spectacular shopping spree, and relatively little interest in the bills that would eventually have to be paid. We are the children of fortune. Who wants to grow up? Yet as we've moved irrevocably toward national adulthood, so too have come the unhappy facts of responsibility, whether or not we are ready, whether or not it seems fair.

We are all quick to point fingers at each other. Whites blame blacks and blacks blame whites. Women blame men and men blame women. Suburbanites blame city-dwellers, Democrats blame Republicans, conservatives blame liberals, managers blame laborers who blame managers, parents blame kids who blame parents.

It's a whole lot easier than digging your heels in, taking responsibility, making a stand. That requires work and commitment. It also means accepting that life isn't fair, or as easy as the ideal we've been sold.

Bob Echols, his wife Ann and I were tucked into a good meal at a nice restaurant near their home in east Texas, the night we met and started to examine the meaning of success. I'd found the couple through Amway, a home products company that promises wealth, independence and pyramid dreams. Though skeptical, I was also curious about this uniquely American enterprise. I was prepared for plenty of rhetoric and not a lot of heart or help in my ongoing research on the subject of happiness. As is almost invariably the case when I prejudge a story, my presumptions were wrong.

"What we need is a little self-respect," said Echols, starting out pretty much as I would have expected. "If you can give people their self-respect and let them know that it's all right to do better, to work hard in life, then they will.... But in the society we live in today, a lot of people have lost their dreams and aren't even aware of it. They don't know what it is to feel sure, to get in the game with all they've got."

The Echols were both on their second marriages, highly successful and proud of their gorgeous white home and its acres of land. They were jauntily dressed, a handsome pair who seemed enraptured to have come so far. Bob, fifty-three, had been raised in a hardscrabble homestead at Kildare Junction. It was just his daddy and him, running wild hogs, fishing, chasing rabbits and coaxing juicy watermelons from the ungiving East Texas ground. Ann's had been a more conventional childhood, a small-town Catholic upbringing that included typing skills and making good grades. There was no money for college, so she did what a lot of young women of her generation did: got married and helped put her first husband through school. She tried not to mind doing the bookkeeping at a furniture store. She accepted that she would not become an archeologist or attorney, as she'd dreamed. "Growing up, I always wanted to make something of myself. I look at kids today and they're not concerned with what their parents think of them. But I wanted to make mine proud," said Ann, incongruously steely and soft all in pastels.

The Echols were big boosters of Amway, working not only as distributors but also recruiters for the multi-billion-a-year direct sales company whose zealous free enterprise philosophy and motivational meetings many find off-putting. This couple, though, had found sheer liberation, and a strong sense of home, in selling soaps and other household products.

"The opportunity has been unlimited," said Bob, his sharp, blue eyes the only real clue to the shrewd businessman behind the warm hound-dog face. "Without education, special friends or political pull I've had a beautiful life, traveled all over the world." Added his wife: "There may be other vehicles out there. But this is the one I—*we*—found. It's not a cure-all vehicle. Some succeed and some fail, like in anything else. But we've been able to build a million-dollar business."

It was a long way from 1969, when Bob Echols had two dozen W-2 forms and callouses from as many welding, pipe-cutting, carpentry and oil roughnecking jobs up and down the Mississippi River. Long a diehard Democrat—"You might say socialistic, even communistic,"—he was disillusioned with his union, "bitter at the system" and tired of sharing a ten-foot trailer home with his first wife, four young kids and miscellaneous relatives. The marriage was troubled and his prospects for prosperity decidedly bleak. Echols had no higher education or connections. He didn't even have a set of decent clothes to wear on job interviews. He had nothing to lose when a friend asked him to an Amway recruitment meeting. "I figured I could earn a few extra bucks," he said.

With Horatio Alger style, Echols did a lot more than that. "It goes back to truth," Bob said, "having somebody to tell you like it is; someone who will tell you to get off your ass, by God, because you're accountable. I had a sense that I was accountable for the course of my life."

Accountability. The word can be lumped with a bunch of other "old-fashioned" terms, the kind that grandparents use to the groans of their grandkids around the

Christmas dinner table. Words like *discipline* and *responsibility*, *good citizenship* and *sacrifice*. Words like *justice* and *morality*. What a shame that they sound so dated and corny, thanks to the patronizing way in which liberals have for years relegated them to some sort of reactionary, unhip zone even as their do-good intentions fail, often insult, the disadvantaged members of society they presumably wish to support. What a shame, too, and no less so, that conservatives have co-opted these words and confined them to the narrowest of definitions, using them to judge and exclude huge swaths of society in a spirit that seems neither Christian nor democratic.

America was founded on the principle that individuals have certain inalienable rights, among them the freedom to determine their own religious, moral and political beliefs within the bounds of law. It is a fairly simple formula, which is perhaps why it's one of history's most remarkable achievements. But corny or not, and regardless of our insecurities, a few essential strings are attached.

"I had a teacher growing up who told me I was never going to be good for anything more than ditch-digging," Echols said. "And that felt terrible. I doubted myself. Couldn't help it. But still, I knew it was up to me. I had to make something of my life. No one was gonna do it for me." As her husband recounted his story, Ann Echols listened, rapt and protective of her life partner and friend. Like her pink sweater, delicate ballet slippers and tasteful coiffure, the couple's capitalist dream seemed nearly airbrushed to perfection. They were so solid, so sure in a world where nothing truly is. They were two people whose lives hadn't worked all that well apart. Together, they'd built a business and prosperous life.

Think whatever you wish about Amway. The Echols didn't particularly care. They had worked hard and earned for themselves a certain level of comfort. It was theirs. Their sense of ownership and security was clear. But even for all their hard work and success, mysterious fate made no guarantees.

The night had worn on, the dishes had been cleared and we were all about talked out. Then, over a last cup of coffee, Bob Echols leaned forward and dropped his voice. "My son died of AIDS not so long ago," he said.

The boisterous good ol' boy, the ebullient storyteller, had vanished.

"He was twenty-eight," whispered his wife, her face suddenly blank, "a beautiful boy." She had been close with her stepson, had never dreamt that he would leave the world so soon. With well more than a million Americans now testing HIV-positive, it is no longer a disease seen in the distance. It has come into so many unsuspecting homes, touched the lives of so many people who thought themselves exempt. The Echols had worked hard to shape a beautiful world, to build for themselves a glorious haven. There would be no more suffering or confusion in this place. Rational or not, that's what most of us hope for, whatever our particular strategy or plan: that moment when finally we're safe, beyond trouble's reach.

And, of course, life being what it is, we never arrive.

"People blame their unhappiness on God, family, race, you name it. Like any of those things guarantee anything. . . . We live in a fragile world. Whole lives change—poof—just like that. There are no guarantees," said Echols, who was not so much angry as resigned. "Happiness is about dealing with a load of problems you never wanted or expected. It's about staying in the game, even when all the rules change. Happiness is about how well you can get up from your knees."

• • •

The trip to Charlotte, North Carolina, stands out most in my mind because I had a horrendous cold. I really, *really* didn't want to go cover this serial murder case. And I'm afraid all my colleagues heard as much. But there I was, stuffy head stuffier still for the concoction of cold medications I'd taken, wandering toward the police department shortly before dawn on a frigid spring day. I'd flown in late the night before, but thanks to the Sudafed was wide-eyed at 5 A.M. None of the cops wanted to talk to me, and I didn't really blame them. I'd been a local reporter. I knew how grating it was when the "national" media descended, looking for a quick take on stories that inevitably defied any such thing.

In this case, it seemed that a young black man by the name of Henry Louis Wallace had stalked and murdered nearly a dozen young black women over the space of two years. Until recently, the deaths had not been linked, which gave rise to some speculation. Had these women been white joggers in a nicer part of town, would there perhaps have been more coverage in the local paper, more vigilance on the part of police? Hard to know for sure. Easy to suggest diabolical, brazen prejudice when the crimes are laid out in hindsight.

At any rate, this man, Henry Louis Wallace, had now been apprehended. That and gimlet eyes were about all that the cops would give me. So, I figured, get a cup of coffee. And as long as I was at it, why not drive over to the neighborhood where, as far as I understood, all of the murdered women once had drunk theirs. I drove out along a lush, leafy avenue, expecting my destination would be a contrasting study in depression. Instead, I found a pleasant enough area that was far from run-down.

The Bojangles restaurant where four of the strangled women had worked was pretty empty. I got an orange juice and not much of a response from the counter clerks I questioned. "Yeah, we knew them," they said of the dead women. "It's kind of scary."

Settling down over my tray I noticed a young black man absorbed in a book. He didn't look like a good prospect. I figured he would, with reason, rebuff a reporter's questions. Again, my intuition was wrong. Sandifer McCullough was just coming off work, more than willing to talk as he geared up for the rest of his day. He said he was a counselor for juvenile offenders. That was his job. His avocation, his passion, was counseling family, friends and neighbors, because it was all he could think of to do. He was troubled by the serial murders, but not because the alleged murderer was black. Or because his victims were of the same color. He was disturbed because it had taken a heinous crime to draw national attention to his small community, to this place where people were struggling to live decent lives.

"The real point is that black people, not just here but in communities all over the country, are dying in all kinds of ways, every day," said McCullough, finishing up his fast-food breakfast. "My reality is that I'm considered an old man in my community because I'm nearly thirty and I'm not rotting in jail and don't have a bullet through my head. My reality is that sometimes I might just be walking to a Bible study class, and the police will stop me because I'm a black man.... My reality is that they don't show guys like me in the news. They show our young men wearing hoods and handcuffs."

Violence—or the sense of it—is pervasive. Anxiety about it has pushed crime to the top of political agendas, made law-and-order a popular stump-speech theme. But clearly the threat white people perceive is skewed: Blacks, who make up about 12 percent of the population, are the victims in 50 of every 100 homicides committed nationwide, according to recent federal statistics. In this context, the accusations against Henry Louis Wallace were nearly dwarfed. "It's tough to think about, but we as citizens need to think about it that way if we're ever really going to do anything about it," said Harper Wilson, an FBI special agent who helped me with the story.

The daily death toll in the nation's minority communities mostly goes on in silence, newsworthy not so much for its extraordinary upward spiral as for the chilling ordinariness of it all. Disproportionate arrest and murder rates, unemployment, drug abuse, poverty, the daily reality of police brutality and racism are complex and difficult to unravel.

"So the media focus on the exceptions, the glamorous, the macabre, the bizarre, the unique," said Dr. Carl Bell, a Chicago psychiatrist known for his work on race issues. "It's simple-minded, stereotypic, misleading, distorted and certainly isn't helpful."

Reporters are supposed to comfort the afflicted and afflict the comfortable, or so the old saying goes. We are supposed to uncover what stinks, provide a check against imbalance, tell the truth, till the soil, challenge the system to do better. It is a sacred trust, a responsibility usually assumed for the most idealistic of reasons. Frankly, most of us don't get paid enough to do the job otherwise. But somehow the drive to "do good" has gotten mixed up with the chase to "keep up" with tonight's hottest interview, tomorrow's sexiest story. Over and over "average" people have told me that we in "the media" are failing, paying too much attention to all the wrong things, too little attention to the stuff of real American life. Many have felt displaced by a barrage of sound bites that come from self-anointed spokespeople—conservative and liberal—whose agendas they do not share. The stories we tell too often do not illuminate, are dimmed by false images and formulas that are disembodied and disconcertingly abstract. Too frequently we talk in journalese, study only surface dimensions, forgetting the passion and compassion that fuel the truest work. Rather than doing what we're supposed to do—spur necessary and useful conversation—we more often than not go for what's easy or safe, box ourselves into a sterile style that reader and viewer surveys suggest fails to reach the public we allegedly serve.

Fewer and fewer people—especially young people—read any newspaper at all and the TV "news" many get is as likely as not to come from someone who looks like an anchor, sits behind an anchor-style desk, but whose top story is Michael Jackson. Minute-by-minute O.J. Simpson coverage is a long way from the kind of journalism that Edward R. Murrow practiced and to which many in the business still aspire. On the one hand there has been much hand-wringing among the "legitimate" press, concern about credibility and the "dumbing down" of news. On the other, market pressures, new technology and corporate bean-counting have increasingly cultivated a "give-the-people-what-they-want" mentality that only clouds the mission. The news business has changed dramatically over recent years, independently owned newspapers being swallowed up by conglomerates and unique voices eaten away. Cable has exploded, as has access to information on-line. More and more people have gone around the traditional media—talking directly to one another via computer bulletin boards, talk radio or call-in TV. In many ways it's enormously exciting, and liberating to many who have felt for some time that the reporters representing them at press conferences were asking the wrong questions, missing the most important points.

The pity is that by drawing into a shell, issuing "the media" a blanket rejection, people may also make themselves part of the problem. Much of what has come to make newspapers fly or fail, newscasts soar or sink, has to do with what the public demands. But sometimes being truly informed requires a different, less comfortable voice. There are troubling things in the world—both at home and abroad—that we might not want to hear about but absolutely need to know. In order to make decisions, in order to agitate for necessary change, citizens must have information—real information, not the type to be found on tabloid TV. Nor is it enough simply to listen to ourselves and the totally like-minded individuals who call our favorite radio hosts. Being well-informed means at the very least examining, sometimes accommodating, other points of view. That's what the healthiest democratic dialogues are all about—hashing out difficult problems, challenging each other to see in new ways. It's a process that "the media" are supposed to help facilitate, a discourse that thousands upon thousands of citizens want to have, but sadly it's a discourse on which they can't depend.

Sandifer McCullough urged me to go down to the center of town where a vigil against violence had been held at noon each day over many months. It wasn't part of my prepackaged deadline account of serial murder, he said, but it was the heart of a more penetrating tale. "Just check it out," he said. "Do it for me."

So I did, wandering among sharply tailored men and women who had tumbled out of their office buildings for a sunny lunchtime stroll. Where was this vigil? I was waiting for something along the lines of a New York demonstration featuring the flamboyant likes of the Rev. Al Sharpton trailed by a horde of hungry newshounds. Minutes ticked by. My deadline was growing closer. I couldn't see any story. Then came the slightly stooped figure of Eddie Byers, dressed all in black, decidedly out of step with the suits shuffling purposefully by. Very quietly, imperceptibly if you weren't watching out, he bowed his head and stood very still. In time he was joined by a few other regulars, and together they joined hands in a brief, quiet prayer against black-on-black crime.

That was all there was to it.

The brutal truth was that Henry Louis Wallace was only one black man, and the young black women he was accused of strangling were mere additions to an already lopsided set of grim statistics mirrored nationwide. Of a record 122 homicide victims in Charlotte the year before, 94 victims had been black, like roughly 70 percent of those who had been charged with violent crimes over the same stretch of time.

"You take a person like Mr. Wallace and, well, there's so much killing, so much crack cocaine going on, he's just another grain of sand on the beach," said Byers, who described himself as being "from the streets."

And so, each day at noon, he and a small band of others came to pray.

Robert Walton, a county commissioner, was also present. Like Michael Justice, a young waiter, he had come to meditate on change. Sometimes, they said, only one or two people showed up. On good days, there were more. But never enough, the men said. "It will take so many more to repair what's wrong," Walton explained before bowing to lead a final prayer. "Lord, we need healing in this here land," he intoned as people streamed by in twos and threes, black and white, bits of their conversations carried by the midday breeze. No one stopped to ask what the men were doing.

"No one ever does," Justice said. "Until something happens, like a Henry Wallace. That's when people have questions. After the fact."

• • •

Reporters, politicians, talk-show hosts and the like may highlight the bizarre, the shocking, unusually heartbreaking or heartwarming. But we all know there is so much more out there, so much texture less easily defined. I live in New York City, a place known primarily for its excesses and extremes: richness and poverty, glamour and depravity. Like so many other images we hold of ourselves, all of this is projected through the prism of movies and television and news reports that do not capture much of reality. They do not capture the lives lived in between: People like my neighbors, people like the Korean grocer who runs tabs for local shoppers or the Latino busboy who stops sweeping the sidewalk to put a quarter in a panhandler's jangling cup. They don't notice the city bus driver who honks at 10 P.M. each evening to let a doorman friend know it's time to catch his ride home, do not see Central Park on a summer's evening when tens of thousands of people listen to symphony music while spread out on blankets under imaginary stars. The sweeping brushstroke misses my friend Ram Singh, an Indian immigrant who dispenses political commentary along with the daily papers he hawks near the B-train at dawn. The broad camera pan does not linger on Ensley "Woody" Woods, a toothless octogenarian who watches and waves as the rest of the hurried world whips by to work each morning.

The thing about America is that anywhere you go—Paducah, Kentucky, for instance—only a bit of digging will turn up gold. Heroes are there to be found, everywhere. They just don't make headlines.

One such hero is Anthony Gwynn, a guy I've interviewed over and over but have never properly used in an AP story. I guess he's never done or said anything "special" enough, or especially heinous. We met on a street corner the first time I happened into Paducah. It was in one of the city's sadder sections. I was lost. Striding along at a good clip, he was a welcome contrast to the other residents listlessly lolling out in front of their low-slung, low-income buildings. A string of multicolored charms loaded down the keychain he swung in one hand, Narcotics Anonymous markers for his weeks and months of sobriety. He was purposefully headed somewhere, but made time to talk.

"I'm a recovering addict," he offered almost immediately. "I used to see everything through the eyes of addiction." He used to see everything, he said, through the lens of his own immediate needs. Gratification was the bottom line, and the quicker the better. For about seven or eight years, he wasn't even sure anymore exactly how long, Gwynn hadn't given a damn. Until one day, just like that, he reached the limit. He got tired of the hustling, "tired of being sick and tired all the time." And so he started talking, relentlessly looking for new places to go. He talked to members of a support group, and he talked to people on the streets.

It was hard to imagine him as a lowlife. As cars drove by that first day we got to talking out on the street, one local after another had a thumbs-up sign to offer or kind word to say. Gwynn had become a sort of one-man self-help network, badgering kids to stay off the drugs, helping old friends find their way back to steadier ground. He'd been clean and sober fifteen months when we first met. It has been twice that long now. "I talk with people that want a way out, and I say, 'What lengths are you willing to go to, how hard are you willing to work?'" he said. "Everybody's ready. I see their mouth working, but I ain't seen their feet going nowhere. . . . You can sit here at night and see fifteen, sixteen-year-olds hustling for two, three dollars to get their fix. They don't think they're at the bottom. I don't know what they're thinking. People from other countries take jobs for two, three dollars an hour. But we don't want to start at the so-called bottom. We want someone to give us eight, nine dollars an hour and if [the job] is two blocks away and it's raining out, we don't want to go. We have to humble ourselves.

"People in America today don't know how to accept pain. . . . Hey, I'm a baby boomer," said Gwynn, who was a little over thirty. "Everything is about self—me, me, me. I don't care if you're white, black, whatever. If your ass is capable, you should be out there. They asked me when I first went into Narcotics Anonymous to change, and that meant change everything."

I thought of William Bell, the homeless man I'd seen through some stunning changes after he was finally ready to leave the neighborhood block where he'd made a decent living panhandling among my soft-touch Upper West Side neighbors. Change. It was a word he also used a lot. "I've gone through so many changes," he had said repeatedly throughout his recovery. "I had to change my whole way of thinking," he had said time after time.

Change is a long, difficult process.

But slowly, because Bell and Gwynn and countless others had been willing to take up the challenge, they'd climbed out of that lying place that promised bliss in a bottle, or in any other of the drugs people use, mind-altering or not. They had given up the false, swaggering image of themselves as tough and untouchable, the men on the street. Watch Gwynn today coaching Little League kids. Though there aren't any immediate highs, no escape from whatever is getting him down, he has found some things that are more potent than pain, more gratifying than the possibility of some brief escape.

The last time I saw Anthony Gwynn, we met at a sort of fern bar on Paducah's nicest strip. I was exhausted by my efforts to understand a murderous carjacking spree, failing to get a grasp of the true subtext of the story. Why had these young men done it? What had led the way? Our meeting was really just for old time's sake, but quickly my new-old friend fell to sharing some of his straight-talking insights. The word on the street, he said, was substantially different from anything my law enforcement sources had said. There was talk of conspiracies and supremacist schemes, of drug connections and more than a passing connection between the alleged killers and a white victim who by all accounts was totally pristine.

As Gwynn reeled off predictions about whether or not the young men charged would go to trial or plead to some crime, he toyed pensively with the ice in his Coke. In his community, life worked by a set of rules entirely different from those used by judicial officials. The accused boys were not looking simply at jail time. "Twenty years, fifteen years, to a guy who's sixteen years old, it's all the same. It's life." Gwynn wasn't playing a violin for these boys, whose guilt or innocence he could not judge. He was talking about the streets, the meanness that had stolen hope from so many of his friends. Our conversation soon strayed from the particulars of the case. The boys involved weren't boys Gwynn could look at in isolation. His was a longer view. "I just basically care about people who care. But for a lot of people, there's no sense of that left. That's why I love coaching the Little League. There's this unconditional love, honesty, bonding. It don't matter if you don't have much athletic skill. It don't matter if you're black or white. It's about communicating. Caring.

"Some people think they can do it all on their own. Me? I don't believe in will-power. I believe in a power greater than myself. It ain't got nothing to do with religion. It's spiritual, but it's also just about being responsible for yourself."

The news media didn't have much to do with Anthony Gwynn or the kids he was teaching out on the ball field. No cameras were there when he walked to work in the morning or when someone dangled a temptation that he steadfastly declined. But there he was, nonetheless, a pillar, a person on the streets of Paducah who offered guidance to junkies who wanted out, support to children without parents, hope to teenagers for whom role models were in short supply.

Gwynn was more alone than he wanted to be. He'd looked out, found that connections and commitment were far more life-giving than the code of the streets. But too few of his peers were there with him. There's this whole world of young people to save, he said, a universe of people who have not committed to the fight.

After we'd finished our sodas, Gwynn took me on a walk down by the waterfront. A big quilt show had drawn thousands of aficionados to town, but things were still pretty quiet. We sat for awhile on a bench by the Ohio River. I thought about quilting, about America as a big blanket made of so many small pieces. I don't know what Anthony was thinking. More time went by. Eventually he asked, "What do you hear?" I said that I heard a barge steaming by, the chirp of a few happy birds, the sound of a family laughing down the promenade.

He asked again, "But what do you *hear*?"

I said I heard nothing and that it was peaceful. I said that I heard some extraneous noise but that it was a murmur compared with the streets of New York. He looked at me as if he knew something more than I could offer. He looked at me without saying a word, and for so long that I grew slightly awkward, uncomfortable. "We all hear what we hear, wouldn't you say?" he offered. "I won't criticize what you hear or don't hear."

As we walked back into the shopping district, I felt somehow I'd failed. I wanted to be deep, to understand what he did about the troubles eating at black communities, the forces at work among the drug-addicted, the impoverished, the outsiders, the struggling stragglers. He told me not to be stupid. I couldn't understand. I wasn't one of them.

"But you can be uncomfortable. We all should be. There are a lot people like you, who are uncomfortable with things they don't understand. So they make noise. Turn in a different direction, look away. The difference is, a lot of people, they have nowhere to go. They can't escape. When they hear nothing, that's the sound of their lives, their feeling of value. Nothing. Silence."

Here, he said, in this place of silence lies the ringing question: How, when, where do we begin?

• • •

Some decades ago, there was a train stop, a skating rink, a movie theater, a big general store and two car dealerships in Dongola, Illinois, population 535. Nearby you'd have found a flour mill and a chicken hatchery. The town really bustled back then. That, Hallie Hinkle said, was a good time. Now, the beautifully crinkled great-grandmother said, everything was different. "It's kind of sad here, isn't it?" she asked, her flat tone all but answering the question.

And I had to say yes, it was kind of sad. Still, driving by chance into Dongola, I'd come quickly upon a lively group of toddlers at play, among them one of Mrs. Hinkle's tribe. Her newest great-grandchild belonged to Laura Pratt, a daughter-in-law fresh from New York. Other young mothers were cautious, standoffish when a stranger arrived in their midst, but not Mrs. Pratt. She spoke right up. And between her and her remarkable Grandma Hallie's caring and wit, there lay the hope of rekindled small-town spirit. They were adults, making their way.

Laura Pratt did not want to live in a dying place. She would not let her daughter grow up in or be closeted by the shadow of a pale, half-forgotten place. "With the economy and all, I guess everybody's watching out for their own selves," said the brunette, who was barely twenty-seven. "And it's sad, because when you have teamwork, you at least have a chance." Her smile was sunny, her laugh infectious. In minutes she'd hooked me up with friends all around town. "See over there?" she said, "That's a young guy who's starting up a business. And over there?" she continued, pointing farther down the town's only commercial block. "That's the Dinner Bell. I waitress there sometimes and so do some of my friends."

The town was populated largely by the families of truckers, men who stopped home to visit and then quickly left on long trips to elsewhere. Mrs. Pratt was one such half-time widow, which made it especially nice that Grandma Hallie was around to offer support. When Roy was on the road, Laura could still count on a family gathering around the old homestead table. Between her brothers-in-law and their extended families, she could always find someone in the mood to touch base and swap stories over dumplings or pie. "You know, I think people are tired of being alone," she said one afternoon. "If you pull together you can really have something. But it takes work, people holding it together."

In small towns where the morale is on empty, it's not an easy order. A little later, gathered around iced teas at a corner table in the Dinner Bell, several mothers who also waited tables mused on what had made it so hard.

"They say people were happy in the Depression," said Kelly Gaddis, thirty-two, who had a couple of kids. "People stayed at home. They had, what? Perspective, I guess you'd say. And in a way, maybe that's what we're going through. For a long time nothing was ever good enough, big enough. But now, just about anything's OK. It makes me sad, but maybe it's not so bad." Maybe, all the women gathered that day agreed, it was about time that American assumptions and priorities got the good shake-up they needed.

We've hung out a lot of dirty laundry, and the airing has been long-overdue. It was about time that we started confronting wife battery and addiction, homosexuality, child neglect and sexual abuse, racism, sexism, injustice and suffering of all kinds. I've heard great relief in the voices of people who at long last discovered it was neither weak nor shameful to seek healing and support. The problem is, it's possible for the pendulum to swing too far. To many, our quest for self-knowledge has come to feel a bit like an extended belch of self-absorption. Enough with the mass victimization, with a syndrome an old friend of mine calls the "poor-little-old-me's." We've got serious work ahead, a nation and vision to save. Maybe we don't need a whole lot more self-understanding and acceptance.

Maybe what America really needs—even craves—is a good dose of "tough love."

"People are getting back down to home and family, bringing themselves back to reality. Having a sense of yourself is important. But basically, life's just a lot of work. I think a lot of us have only started figuring that out in the last five or so years. It's reality-check time. People are staying home more. They're looking for some stability, quality. Forget the Nintendo games," said Mrs. Pratt, who had all but exiled TV from her home. "You wouldn't eat out of a garbage can, so why put it in your head? You have to be in the world—not watching it—to care."

Just across from the park where the young mothers had gathered that morning was Chris West, who had come in early and would be working late. This small shop, after all, was his ticket to a better future. It was a junk store, the kind of place where customers might barter this old couch for that new table. Like Pratt, he was twenty-seven. Young and absolutely determined to succeed.

"There's a line being drawn. There are some who are going to fight to make things better and others who are going to go deeper in the hole," he said. "I'm going to be a father. I know I can accomplish anything and my kids will know it, too. There's got to be a whole lot of cleaning up, though. Too much garbage. We've got too much garbage of all kinds: Pollution. Attitude. Unions. Companies. You can see the factories closing down and people out there saying 'I thought this was going to be easy.' People are tired of sitting in the dumps and waiting for something to be handed to them. . . . We've seen some hard times. OK. Now maybe we're in the stage where we know work's got to be done. It's a massive adjustment." But it was an adjustment that Chris West, for one, was willing—even eager—to make.

Laura Pratt takes some time out with her daughter, Michelle, on their front porch in Dongola, Illinois.

"In a way it makes me think of that movie, *Schindler's List*," Mrs. Pratt said, sometime later. After seeing the film about how one man, Oskar Schindler, managed to save hundreds of Jews who might otherwise have died in the Holocaust, "My husband was really shaken up by that movie. It touched Roy's heart. But he also said it depressed him. 'People aren't like that these days,' he said to me. He told me, 'No one today would go out on a limb to save lives the way that man did.'

"But I said to Roy, 'Roy, there *are* people like that. You just have to look for them.'"

Many of us do retreat, choose to look out mostly for ourselves, dismiss suffering that is not our own, distance ourselves from pain we don't understand. It is only human, this impulse to focus on our own best interests.

But maybe our own best interests are ill-served when we draw away from each other. Maybe one by one, as gradually as Schindler himself came to care for the Jews facing death, we are coming to understand that you can't really belong until you get real, look reality square in the face.

Look out across the American landscape—at city blocks that are war zones, at schools in disrepair, at families torn by violence, at children in despair—and see the legacy of compassion and action deferred. Then look at a speck of an Illinois town called Dongola and hear what you can hear in so many others: People making a choice; choosing to join in.

"In small communities there isn't a lot of talk," Mrs. Pratt said. "But it's kind of like something has slapped us in the face and now everybody has a sting mark. We're all trying to figure out how to make it stop stinging. And slowly, maybe, we're figuring out that it's a balance—a balance between what I want and what we all need.

"Instead of sinking," she said, "we all might as well swim."

Getting in the Act 5

True Grown-Ups Aren't Afraid to Play

Over the years, no matter the city or town, I've tried to volunteer, which on the face of it would seem simple enough. But no less than in any other kind of relationship, the commitment to working with and for others takes something more resolute than the intermittent holiday yen. Veteran organizers are often dismissive, I think as a sort of test of the neophyte do-gooder's mettle. In the brusqueness of some I've heard a subtext: "So what's the *real* story? Are you going to stick around in a serious way?" They have a right to ask because, over the long haul, many of us do not. Datebooks get filled up, the novelty wears off, the repeated failures wear thin. The nadir of my own particular quest for a place to do good works came on Thanksgiving 1990, in the basement of Holy Trinity Church in upper Manhattan. A small group of neighborhood women had cooked most of the day, putting together a feast for the homeless men who would soon file in. I was flushed with seasonal spirit and the gentle camaraderie. Our guests would love this cranberry sauce, savor the turkey stuffing. We had more than enough of everything ready to go when the shelter shuttle bus arrived. The small talk was amiable enough as we all settled down, professionals and panhandlers, church women and stragglers, joining hands around mountains of steaming food. Almost immediately I felt like the star of my own Fellini film, the guy at my left carrying on an animated conversation with himself, the one on my right explaining the finer points of pigeon breeding. I chuckled, a little pleased with myself. It was, I thought, a good thing that we volunteers had done.

"Man, I can't eat no more turkey. How many's this now?" came a voice from a far corner of the table.

"Don't ask me. I lost count three turkeys ago."

With two short sentences, these two scraggly guys, the types you could find any day on any street, had ripped my benevolent mask away. It was humiliating. On this holiday, they'd been stuffed with more stuffing than any Thanksgiving bird. They'd been driven from shelter to shelter, plied with so much food that by now they could barely eat. So much food that by this time they could not enjoy it, even if those who had prepared it felt mighty good.

I'd been part of an absurd, complicitous little game, skimming over the surface, trying to get by with one grand, guilty gesture. What a farce. I vowed to myself never to do things this way again. I was going to roll up my sleeves and make a legitimate difference, dammit, find a way to do something day-to-day.

A few weeks later I stopped by a storefront community project known as The Dome. I'd stopped by before, but the overworked counselors weren't solicitous enough. They lacked organization. This was far too haphazard and chaotic for a busy woman like me. Now, though, I was determined. More than that, I was mad. What had I been waiting for? Some kind of gold-embossed invitation? If coordinators at The Dome did not offer me easy access, I would muscle in. If they dropped the ball, I would pick it up and run alone if necessary. And so Ellen and I came to run a teen writer's workshop that has continued now for more than five years. In first starting out, we were among about a half-dozen volunteers, all of whom fairly swiftly drifted away. On many a Saturday morning, we've laughed at the foolishness in our having remained. How stupid were we to drag ourselves out of bed early, give up precious weekend time, in order to feed and bully and trade bad jokes with a bunch of bleary-eyed inner-city kids? But foolish or not, we continued to show up with our deeply flawed course plans, and we've known great satisfaction for having stayed for such a long while. We have whole histories now with young people entering college. We have, I think on good days, even succeeded in altering lives.

Just imagine if the nation waged a war against social decay at home as determinedly as we once stood against Nazism abroad. Just imagine a peer pressure that made apathy as undesirable as smoking has become and community involvement as much a status symbol as the hottest new car. Just imagine if public service were as cool as rap or as macho as Wrestlemania. Just imagine what it might be like if everyday heroes got the same treatment as Hollywood stars. Sure, it's a simple notion, even naive. But maybe a bit more idealism wouldn't be such a bad thing. Maybe we shouldn't laugh at the fact that once upon a time we were entranced by a guy spinning plates.

Certainly cynicism is no worthier an act.

Marilyn came up with the image, and sent us all into hysterics. It was late at night, a bunch of friends shacked up on a holiday weekend at the beach, shifting about and trying to fall asleep on an assortment of uncomfortable cots, sofas and lumpy beds. "Remember Ed Sullivan," she said into the dark. "Remember that guy with those plates? I mean, what was that about?"

We all howled at our collective flashback: black-and-white TV, an anonymous little man frantically whirling plates on so many poles, adding one more, moving back to recharge another. She'd hit upon what I've come to think of as the "spinning-plate theory of life."

Of course, there is the easy metaphor. What else do we do from day to day but try to keep this or that plate purring along? Rush back to make sure the last one spun isn't outpacing the others, then double back one more time just as this plate wobbles, that one teeters at the brink. If you speed the music up, the dance becomes almost desperate. Slow it down and the whole delicate enterprise threatens to crash down on the floor. That's life.

But what we really got to talking about that night was the idea of a nation tuned in to watch this kind of corny spectacle. Could it have been in our lifetime that this was enough, that this was entertainment? Did families really gather on Sunday nights to watch seals honk horns? Could a variety program that spanned opera to Sinatra to the Beatles from week to week make it in an age when everyone has their own TV? Today offers us so many more options, so many more plates to be spun. We don't need to gather in one living room when cable is hooked up to every room, when computers offer us a million individual rooms, so many separate worlds into which to retreat. It's progress and, in the American culture, progress is generally regarded as good. But somehow in moving forward, some vital part of ourselves got left back. With a zillion videos to be rented, geegaws to be bought, fast-action thrills to be had, watching a guy spinning plates seems as silly and unsophisticated as, well, a guy spinning plates.

This mentality is easy to pin on young people. But it has also been evident in the lives of their parents, their elected officials, the stars most celebrated and tough guys most revered. Dignity and quiet good works, everyday heroes like teachers and community organizers, don't make hot copy or sizzle on MTV. From time to time I've heard people like basketball star Michael Jordan or pop star Michael Bolton or talk-show host Arsenio Hall talk about the importance of being committed, sharing the wealth and creating opportunity for those who are lost. And it's nice to hear. But somehow the message doesn't quite catch on. Such commitments don't work when here and then gone, left to flawed government programs and isolated bands of hard-working volunteers battling the tide. They succeed only on the largest of scales, when huge numbers of people decide to join in. Civic pride and responsibility has not caught fire in the popular imagination.

What is required is a wholesale psychic shift.

The trend-meisters have dubbed the '90s a modest era, one adjusted against the excesses of that *Dynasty*- and *Dallas*-dominated decade we called the '80s. Too many people have been laid off—especially white-collar people—and too many credit cards maxed out, too many boomers have had children, and busters found that "reality bites" for anyone to think that mindless me-firstism is socially acceptable at this point. Political correctitude has set in with a vengeance. And as its opposite there is plenty of knee-jerk counterbombast, equally silly, simple and self-inflated. I heard Rush Limbaugh do a radio promo the other night in which he called himself "the howitzer of truth on the battlefield of ideas." He bills himself as

"on loan from God" and to my ears isn't entirely joking.
Whatever.

We have all these pronunciations, self-conscious rhetoric both from the left and the right, but the real elbow grease necessary to turning things around is far harder to find. President Clinton has sounded themes of family, community, service again and again. But, in part because he never quite seems to stand where he stands, they do not inspire or come across as terribly sincere. Nothing has quite captured the public imagination, galvanized anything approaching a united front, fueled the genuine desire for a common good. There are no clear leaders—and no easy enemies against which to unite. It's just us, a disparate bunch of people with millions of private wounds coming slowly to understand that no one is going to fix America for us, or prescribe one easy-to-swallow pill.

• • •

In theory, people are more closely connected today than ever before. What used to take days or weeks by overland mail now takes seconds by fax. Slowly, then suddenly, millions of people have eased onto the information superhighway, linking themselves to a seemingly infinite community of potential cyberspace friends. Afternoon talk shows lay out all the nation's dirtiest secrets, the sort of personal laundry that used to be hidden indoors. Family therapy and counseling, no longer a province solely of the rich, have enhanced communication in countless American homes. Cheap long-distance rates and budget travel have afforded more people more contact than ever before.

So for all this interconnectedness, all the tools that theoretically might bring us closer in touch with others, why do so many citizens feel so hopelessly left out? It is a theme, a recurrent complaint among people I've talked with over the years. Somehow, no matter the topic of the story at hand, conversations always come around again to a certain emptiness, a nagging feeling of loneliness among citizens of a country that seems ever larger, even as the wider world retracts.

Shortly after Los Angeles was shaken by a mighty earthquake in early 1994, I roamed among the badly damaged neighborhoods surrounding the epicenter. People were skittish, aftershocks sending those who were still able to get into their homes quickly outdoors again. The stuff of everyday rhythms, like morning commutes on the Santa Monica Freeway and grocery shopping at the nearby supermarket, had been smashed.

The lines at emergency relief centers stretched on for blocks. Phone service was still spotty, water in short supply, places to sleep hard to find. Children stuck close to their parents. The threat of looting and violence was not far from anyone's mind. And so I found it a bit surprising to get a jolly wave from a woman collapsed on her lawn chair out behind the rubble of a modest stucco house. "She must have me mistaken for someone else," I thought, waving back tentatively. As I got closer, she asked if I wanted a soda, seemingly oblivious to the fact that we were utter strangers. And so I came to know the Yafi family and their neighbors, the Kims. People like these are without doubt the finest part of my job.

Before the devastation, their lives had been parallel in so many ways: two couples with immigrant dreams, each with two children, two sets of live-in relatives and two-story houses with side-by-side yards. They'd also shared something else: a wall in between. It wasn't a big wall or a mean wall. Just several feet of cinderblock and cement, the kind that line many Los Angeles homes and perhaps separate as many neighbors. Now, though, walls everywhere had tumbled down.

Out of their personal debris, the Yafis and Kims had yanked something new. In merging their separate but parallel lives these two families had found something stronger. They were now two families united as one.

"Before it's just 'Hello. How are you?' Now is different. We're like a family now," said Jeong-seon Kim, smiling at the Yafis as they smiled back. "We was scared. We didn't know what I can do, but they help us a lot."

They had helped each other through days and nights of camping out behind what was left of their ravaged houses, peering in through glass sliding doors at shards of what once had been their everyday lives: mounds of cookware, broken dishes and condiment bottles, books and keepsakes strewn across their respective living room floors, a pile of Kim's son's baseball cards here, a glimpse of the Yafis' crumpled dining room set there.

Jeong-seon Kim and her husband Jaebock, natives of South Korea, had been sharing their gas burner with the Yafis. When Fawaz Yafi and his wife Jacky, natives of Lebanon, were visited by an inspector, they'd made sure that he stopped next door for a look at the Kims' place as well.

"Don't believe governments. Don't believe the big people. Believe people. The small people, the working people. This is the truth of humanity that we learn again and again," said Fawaz, his eyes red-rimmed but sharp. He and his family had seen so much sadness in their native country's slow descent into hell, had taken in so many miles over the years, wanderers in search of a home, a place where finally they could put down roots. Jacky and Fawaz, a multilingual singer who has played club dates around the world, had finally found that place in Granada Hills, an ethnically diverse, working-class suburb a short drive from downtown Los Angeles. They didn't care if this earthquake meant the building would have to begin all over again.

"You look at us," Fawaz said, nodding at his aging mother-in-law. "We are not sad. If it were just us, then maybe. But we are all in it together now, helping each other."

Unlike the majority of people, the Yafis and Kims had already begun their separate days when the deadly rumbling began at 4:31 A.M. In the darkness at the Kims' house, the family was preparing to join other Assembly of God worshippers for 5:30 A.M. services. Jeong-seon and Jaebock, who runs an auto repair shop, were just stirring. Jeong-seon's mother was already down in the kitchen, making their morning tea. Her father had just risen from bed in the room he shared with his grandsons, Jeong-seon's young children.

The house began to shake. The plaster gave way and bricks rained down on the bed where Jeong-seon's father only minutes before had been asleep. Across the room, the ceiling above her dozing sons' bunk beds remained inexplicably unscathed. The family scrambled downstairs, all of them stumbling over broken glass. Miraculously, no one was hurt.

It was God, Jeong-seon said, who saw them to safety.

Next door, Jacky stood in a towel. Once she was dressed for her early shift at a convenience store, Fawaz would give her a ride. Their teenage daughter was asleep down the hall. Upstairs their son and Jacky's sixty-nine-year-old mother were in one room, her sister and brother-in-law in the other.

The house began to tremble. Thirty years of accumulated treasures, crystal that Jacky's mother had safely brought halfway around the world, crashed to the floor.

Like the Kims, they fled onto Balboa Boulevard.

The smell of gas drifted around them. A broken water main unleashed a torrent so swift that it swept up a car. Moments later, a mighty blast erupted into a fearsome fire two blocks away. It looked like Armageddon, the streets flooded and eerily lit by the flames. "I thought we be finished," Jeong-seon recalled, sniffling from a cold the whole family had caught while sleeping outdoors. "It was the end of the world. It seemed so."

"We cried, we laughed, we cried, we laughed," Jacky said.

"I was so scared," her elderly mother added. "But we are safe."

Now, a week later, these families who had been only cordial neighbors before, swung arms around each while remembering those first terrifying hours. Dogs, cats, parents, children, grandparents and visitors all passed back and forth over the toppled wall. A cacophony of broken English spoken through smiles filled the mild evening air. And everyone agreed it was a pity that disaster had finally brought them together, given them the chance to comfort one another and, in so doing, comfort themselves.

One day, many days after the tremoring had ceased, when the Yafis had brought out the last garbage can full of shattered glass and the Kims had replaced their chimney and secured the roof, the inevitable would happen.

The wall would go up again. But things would never be the same.

"There is a saying I know, 'In disaster maybe you meet strangers and let love go,'" Fawaz said. "The wall doesn't matter. We know each other now. Whether [the wall] is up or down, we are family."

"Nature has said, 'Don't have no more borders. Take

down the borders and make one world,'" Jacky concluded, waving a crisis-excused cigarette she swore would be among her last. "We are not alone. We feel like it sometimes. Maybe a lot of time. But we are not. We are not alone."

This renewed certainty, everyone gathered around a picnic table behind their ruined houses that temperate midwinter day agreed, had made an invaluable difference in their tenuous worlds. Maybe, as so often happens, tragedy had forced their hands. But whatever the catalyst, in the end they had come through this treacherous thing together. In the end, even in their separate but parallel lives, they had not been alone.

• • •

They were a couple of bright, personable guys who had been happy in their careers, guys with no particular complaints or axes to grind. Somehow, though, they had gone out hoping for more than whatever it was life had put on their itineraries. It was as if their train had left on time, but the farther it pulled out on the endless track, the foggier their destinations became.

"Our definition of happiness comes today from TV, music, media, advertisements. So we're all afraid of becoming a community. That's not the message we find. The craving for spirituality has increased, but the avenues . . . they just aren't there," John Bocan, a young man with an easy smile, said one afternoon when I happened into Martinsburg, West Virginia. He'd majored in theology and psychology but had gone to work in a Pittsburgh bank, where the salary and benefits were solid. So when, in his late twenties, Bocan decided to give up the professional thing to become a pastoral minister, "people yelled at me, 'Hey, why are you leaving good money and an excellent future?'"

People thought something was wrong. But he knew better, he said, in coming to work at St. Joseph's parish. "It's not as much money as I got before, but I wouldn't trade this. Money's not the thing. To be in a community, work with other people who have struggles, and acknowledge our faults and strong points, that meant something to me."

The story with Herb Peddicord had been much the same. Heading toward thirty, he'd had a lucrative job as an Army helicopter pilot. He was satisfied with much of his life, except for the nagging notion that "we were put here on earth not to be uniquely separate. We were put here to care for and share with one another."

And so the two young men, each coming by his own path, had ended up working together at a small-town church for a veteran priest they called father. The Rev. William Nolte was made of different stuff, a man shaped by a Depression-era youth and now on the brink of retirement, he was no longer searching so much as assessing the span of his life and priesthood. "It seems we are all victims these days. And if we're not, then we're repressing something," Nolte, sixty-nine, said. "Ever since World War II, the idea of putting on a smile and sacrificing for others has been out of style."

This drew a laugh from his two young colleagues, men who had been hearing mixed messages for some time. "Being part of a community—working with people instead of against them—that's spirituality. That's what's missing: Spiritual peace," said Bocan.

"There's a lot of surface happiness out there. But I think deep down people—especially young people—are just lonely," added Peddicord. "A lot of people feel cut off."

One of the biggest TV spectacles of recent seasons was the final episode of the popular sitcom based in a Boston bar called *Cheers*. The hoopla is hard to recall now, but it was a major deal, prompting endless newspaper columns and one of the biggest viewing crowds of all time. About 2.2 million homes tuned in, but for all the hype the show's last episode was actually poignantly simple. There were no big surprises or soliloquies.

The regular patrons we'd known over ten years did what they'd always done: gathered at a friendly tavern that had been a home away from home. And in saying a final good-bye, they summed up life in a way a lot of people could understand. They had been brokenhearted, had settled for less than they'd hoped, had found the road through life sometimes bumpy and disappointing. But finally, they were all there together. In struggling to define the things most important in life, a conversation I've witnessed at many bars, the *Cheers* crew came up with these: comfy shoes and solid bonds. Hollywood is a lot of the time off-key, but in this the writers and producers seemed to speak to something a lot of us have come to: Having a place where you're welcome, being among people who understand, accepting that nothing is sure but the occasional creature comfort and kinship—family in all its various forms. These were the things that secured small, life-affirming triumphs in a world that often feels lonely and insecure.

In writing this book, I checked back with some of the people with whom I'd fallen out of touch, the men of St. Joseph's in particular. Panic spread through me when the new parish priest said it would be better if I skipped mentioning them. All were gone now, he said a bit ominously, and left it at that. I wondered whether Father Nolte had somehow retired in disgrace or whether John Bocan and Herb Peddicord had not been so altruistic as they seemed.

I set to work tracking them down, which wasn't hard.

They were still living nearby, still loosely tied to St. Joseph's church. But time's passage and a new regime had moved them along. Budget cuts had squeezed the younger men out, and Father Nolte was enjoying his retirement exactly as planned, dividing his time between caring for a troubled parish in Haiti and working for a state correctional program. "Other than that, I'm praying for some understanding of God's plan," he joked, sort of. "You know," he then said, growing a little serious, "that's the whole thing in a way. We want to know what's going on but we can't. Not truly. We don't want to be alone, and yet we are. And yet we get up each morning anyway. If you have something—anything that means something in life—you keep getting up again."

When I caught up with John Bocan, it turned out he'd gone back to his hometown of Pittsburgh after being laid off at the parish only to return some months later to Martinsburg "because there were people here who cared about me and were concerned." Both Bocan and Herb Peddicord, who was now married and a new father, had found work at a local bookbinding factory where the titles they helped produce included self-help and inspirational bestseller's like former U.S. Secretary of Education William Bennett's *Book of Virtues* and the movie spin-off handbook *Gumpisms*.

"I guess we're part of this thing called 'Generation X,'" said Bocan, who had recently turned thirty. "I have many friends who have gone through college and done well and are working at McDonald's now. What we need to do—unlike our parents who found jobs and made lifetime careers—we need to be willing to adapt to change, and very quickly. But sometimes I wonder if we human beings are equipped to do that. I sometimes refer to myself as a nomad. And many of us are. But the nomads who used to roam the Middle East picked up and moved their whole communities, whereas we're out there on our own. That promotes a cult of individualism—an 'I'm gonna get mine' mentality—that leaves a lot of us just feeling really, really lonely.

"I'd like to think the majority of us are willing to help make things better," Bocan said the last time we spoke. "But let's put it this way: For all the TV and media hype, people still can't seem to situate themselves. Trying to get people involved has always been a problem, but it's even more difficult these days. Even though we are all feeling it, the cutting edge of trouble, we are shortsighted. We still don't know that we're all involved in some way—whether we think so or not."

• • •

I'm not a terribly "good" Catholic. Not, at least, in the strictest sense. Though I've never left the church entirely, I've had problems with it since adolescence—those years when I decided it would be just as valid to commune with God in nature, preferably while spending Sundays at the beach. My mother nixed this plan. The least I could do, she said, was sit myself down in the pew for an hour once a week and count my blessings. Even, she said, if I didn't agree with—or bother listening to—the sermon being preached. If it was inconvenient or uncomfortable, well, all the better. That was partly the point and it made some sense to me, so as a college student dabbling with agnosticism and later, in foreign towns where the Mass was said in languages I didn't speak, while living in parishes where the religious values weren't quite my own, more often than not I've attended church on Sunday mornings, ever on the lookout for some transformative pearl.

It has always been pretty much hit-or-miss. Ever since

my eighth-grade Confirmation, which the nuns billed as that moment when God would reach down and definitively touch my soul, I've been waiting. But when the fancy archbishop in his ceremonial dress reached out his hand that day, years ago, and I knelt in anticipation of—what?—some sign that I'd been touched, I found only silence. And pageantry. And no sense of communion, no sense of anyone at my side. To this day, in many ways, I am waiting still. It's only every so often that a little light glints through.

Some months ago, on a Manhattan day so deep in summer that the Mass had to be moved from the unairconditioned church upstairs to the bare, air-conditioned community center below, the Reverend Joseph Koterski gave a remarkable sermon. Or so it seemed to me, given the work I'd been doing. The basement room smelled vaguely of boiled chicken, a remnant perhaps of the endless meals cooked for homeless men who slept there a few nights a week on cots lined in rows, a toothbrush and towel laid on each pillow. Parishioners in shorts and T-shirts, grandmothers and children, Latinos and Haitians, African-Americans and Asians and whites, we were all pressed together on folding metal chairs, singing without an organ, taking communion at a makeshift altar draped in cloth that was plain white. It was all very well suited to the day's theme. Father Koterski's sermon began with the story of a pilgrimage he'd made as a young priest-in-training more than a decade before. He'd been asked to walk 100 miles with nothing, depending like Christ and his disciples once had on the generosity of strangers. As his destination, the young priest chose a shrine kept for the Virgin Mary in eastern Pennsylvania, not far from his childhood home. And so he set out with only a sleeping bag, the clothes on his back and some apprehension about where he might rest, what he might eat in the days to come.

"What was magnificent was that I never went hungry, never felt alone," Father Koterski said in recounting his story. He was never denied food or nourishing conversation, never given a cold shoulder when in need of shelter or direction. People had shared meals from their tables, welcomed him to camp on their land. Caught one night in a ferocious rain, he slept peacefully in a chicken coop out on a farm.

"Given the opportunity, people extended a hand to a stranger," the priest recalled for an audience that seemed extraordinarily engaged. "No one ever let me down."

In some sense, this had been true for me as well. For however much people mistrust—even loathe—"the media," I'd been welcomed again and again. Why, I'll never quite be sure. Perhaps it was naiveté. More likely, I think, it was the overriding impulse most people feel to do what's asked whenever possible, to try to do what's right.

The Bomier family was among so many who allowed a stranger into their home. I was doing a series on community in America and, in putting together a jigsaw map of places I might visit, they played a part. Gae Bomier and I had spoken about what she felt was a renewed sense of commitment to family and neighborhood during a telephone interview on a totally different subject more than a year before. But I'd made a mental note and, when the decks were cleared, called her up in hopes of a follow-up conversation.

"Why, of course. You've got to come out and visit," she said.

Without ever having met me, Mrs. Bomier offered the guest room in her family's suburban Detroit home.

A few hours after I showed up at her front door some weeks later, I asked Mrs. Bomier what had possessed her, why she had made such an offer. She wasn't quite sure. It had just seemed the right thing to do at the time. "I knew that when I actually saw your face I'd know if it was all right. I don't know. I guess that seemed like enough." Their doors opened onto a subdivision in Clarkston, Michigan. It was not exactly the rural snapshot the couple, who had lived previously outside of Washington, D.C., had had in mind. Through years as military "tumbleweeds," they'd dreamed of building a place out in the woods near a lake. Something unique and cozy, with roots custom made. When Barry Bomier retired and shifted back into the private sector, they figured the life they'd imagined would finally be possible. Along the way, though, the finances hadn't quite worked out. And with a school year fast approaching, the Bomiers' two young daughters needed a stable base. So they went with a priced-to-moved builders model "in the kind of place we said we wouldn't be caught dead living in," Mrs. Bomier laughed.

What the family found in time was all they had truly sought: a sense of community.

Their home sat on an acre-and-a-half of what had once been a farmer's field, their property marked by where the lawn abruptly stopped and the unsold, unmowed parcel beyond began. A few kids rode by on bikes the gentle autumn evening I visited, a dog trailing close behind. From the back porch, it was easy to spot neighbors unloading groceries on this side, drawing blinds on that. As night arrived, lights blinked on.

"It looks like a place to raise kids, doesn't it?" said Mrs. Bomier, who at times had both worked outside the home and been a full-time, stay-at-home mom. "But I think it's hard, whether you're in a 'sub' like this or in a city. People get disjointed, separated from that close-knit feeling." This was a traditional nuclear family, but then again, like most in America these days, it was not. Gae, forty-three, was teaching special education, so she and Barry, who worked for a data systems company, were a dual-earning couple. Their marriage was her second, which put them in another large club of families blending children and ex-spouses. They were close to relatives, but found "a large part of our family is not blood-related," also increasingly common in a transient world.

The couple's commitment to civic improvement, church, children, schools and volunteer activities could be matched in many households. It was perhaps the deliberate quality and degree of their involvement that set them slightly apart. "I've thought a lot about good citizenship, the concept of giving to community," said Barry Bomier, forty-two, who left the military shortly after Operation Desert Storm wound down. "Beyond terms, these things have to be understood in the heart. It's what marriage counselors talk about—the being there, the commitment."

Like many people, the Bomiers said they were frightened for the future, the world their two school-age daughters would know. They were often fatigued, sometimes angry at politicians, the media, the economy. But all those feelings were secondary. Above all, they spoke of determination.

"This is about survival, no less than it was for the pioneers on the plains or the immigrants in wood-hulled boats," said Barry, his blue eyes liquid. "What we do now in our communities will tell our story."

On the first Friday of every month, the Bomiers invited relatives, neighbors and friends to dine at an old kitchen table that once had belonged to Gae's grandmother. It was a family tradition they thought worth reviving, a small gesture with simple food and an ever-fluctuating crowd. "We need to sit down together. We can't just say, 'I feel this void and a yearning to fill it but, well, this is my lot in life,'" Gae said. "No! It's a process of teaching, of learning, of nurturing and caring for one another, instead of me, me, me."

That night I dined at the old kitchen table with the Bomiers and their kids. We said grace, then dove into big plates of lasagna, salad and French bread. After the dishes were cleared, we gathered in the living room, where their younger daughter sat transfixed before the TV. We laughed about how old-fogeyish we'd all come to sound, then dropped into silence as the funniness faded, our thoughts perhaps lingering on the overwhelming problems of racial tension, family dysfunction, job loss, pollution, disease and foreign conflict we'd touched on over the course of the evening.

The next day, when I visited Mrs. Bomier at the public grade school where she was teaching, she brought me to the classroom that was a second home to a young and talented teacher by the name of Julie Matties, who allowed me to sit in. "What is a community?" she asked as her second-graders settled down.

A rambunctious, redheaded girl said it was kind of like a club, "where everyone works together and helps each other out."

"What do you do in a community?" the teacher asked.

"Be nice to each other," a wisp-of-a-brunette offered in a whisper.

"What are some ways of being nice to each other?" Matties prodded.

"By sharing," said a tough-looking little boy.

"Be polite," said a girl named April.

"Try not to fight and argue," added her friend, Jennifer.

The discussion was winding down when the rambunctious redhead said loudly, "It's a safe place to be. That's a community. A place where it's safe."

A bit later, Mrs. Bomier took me to meet the school's principle, Doris Moussea. "I think I see a change," she said. "TV producers are becoming conscious of the violence. They're still doing it, but at least they're conscious. Five years ago, no one even thought of it. Education is on the same plane. I see it in the parents coming in. They know things aren't going the way they should and want to do something. But it's a process of teaching, like in Julie's classroom. You start on that level and teach people how to nurture and care for one another instead of themselves alone. We've gone the other way, and a lot of people found it hollow. Now, of course, there is the challenge to find something truer. And I think people are starting to take those first steps."

Added Mrs. Bomier, my intrepid guide, "There's something about pride that makes people stand tall. It doesn't have to have a political agenda or some kind of social goal. It's more basic than that. . . . There's no big, easy answer. We've got a lot of undoing to do. But if we would stop and say we're going to make a concerted effort to teach all our children about joy and commitment, and about hanging in, that would be something. That would be a really big step."

• • •

"We've lost sight of the idea that you reap what you sow, or you get what you work for," said Harold Carl, superintendent for public schools in Pleasants County, a northwestern chunk of industrial West Virginia tucked between Ohio and Pennsylvania. It was a weekday afternoon and a group of us were crowded into a no-frills room at the local board of education office. "I remember when Nixon referred to the great 'silent majority.' Well, it's true that for whatever reason, mainstream America is one of the least vocal sectors. Sometimes maybe we feel the problems are so large that we can't do anything. One thing we can do though—whether in a rural town or on ten blocks in a city—we can take one patch and make a difference," said Carl's thoughtful assistant, Larry Gainer.

The men gathered that day in a charmless building on the edge of a dusty road had made such a difference, zealously working to turn their school district around. Tired of reading dismal reports on the state of public school education, they'd determined it was time to make a stand. "It's a decision and more people are making it," said Gainer, who had worked especially closely with the local business community in developing academic sponsorships and vocational programs. "More and more people realize that if there's going to be a change, then they have to be part of it."

I'd come to West Virginia to find Fred Krieg, who had recently been named the National Association of School Psychologists school psychologist of the year for his innovative work in developing students' self-esteem. While other school systems were faltering, Pleasants County's had become one of the best in the state and a winner of various top national honors. It had all come about through a heavy, consistent emphasis on public service and partnership, Krieg and his colleagues agreed.

They had rejected trends like the one highlighted by a national Parent-Teacher Association survey that found a large majority of students, parents and teachers laying the blame for educational failure at one another's feet. Citizens here took a different path, nearly everyone shouldering responsibility and getting in on the act: Local businesses sponsored students, students worked closely with their teachers, teachers collaborated with parents, parents incorporated education at home. Vocational programs were developed, drugs and teen sexuality addressed head-on, a summer camp for troubled kids put in place. The school was open to parents, who could use it for continuing education or a place simply to meet. A newsletter dealing with child-rearing issues was founded and a seventy-five-hour community student service requirement added to the high school's agenda. Instead of finger-pointing, they developed tools that would point the way for children growing up among struggling factories and idle mines, generations preparing to move into an economy drastically different from the one their parents once knew. They would need solid skills, steady confidence and vision to compete—even thrive—in this evolving world.

"You see more and more articles about murder, kids taking guns to school. We tend to build walls up a little higher, turn away from the problems," said Carl, the superintendent. "I really have been concerned about the moral and ethical fiber . . . the permissiveness in our society. You can worry about it, complain about it, but when it comes down to it what we all really have to do is create alternatives."

It looked to me like they were on the right track. Though the middle-school corridors Krieg and I strolled were standard issue, they were still palpably different from those in similar schools I'd visited around the country. It wasn't just the absence of graffiti and metal-detectors. It was the presence of a certain purpose and energy. It emanated from the classrooms in which laughter could be overheard and glinted in the eyes of teachers and students alike as they made their way along the institutional halls.

Krieg was a hands-on sort of guy, his infectious passion

perhaps fueled by having battled back a virulent cancer not long before. At forty-seven, he was more aware than most that time is something wasted only by cynics and fools. "Everybody wants the easy way," he said, as animated as an evangelist with about a million souls to save. "The people making the decisions are too often the product of a do-it-now-get-rich-quick idea of America. Solutions take time, but we have an America that believes in instant miracles."

In the pouring rain we headed over to—where else?—the local McDonald's for a bit of fast-food lunch. The place was jammed with damp kids yanking at their mothers' skirts, local businessmen in short-sleeved shirts and pastel ties, retirees with coffee slowly to sip, cigarettes to puff on, time to kill. "There's this idea that it's not what you do, but who you are. Well, that's bull," Krieg said, wolfing down a Big Mac between swigs of soda. "You are in fact, at least to some extent, what you do."

We were joined by Chuck Mason, a sharp, young editor for the local weekly. He'd been on staff at a city newspaper, doing the typical young urban professional thing, until it occurred to him several years back that his life was in disorder. His marriage was unhappy and his gut in knots. He'd felt disconnected from the streets he covered and frustrated by the politics that seemed to hog-tie any hope of real civic improvement. It was time for a serious change, which took shape in the form of divorce, remarriage, relocation and a whole new focus. His life now was centered on his second wife, whom he'd met at church, and the children each brought to their marriage. His career now was about community journalism, putting out the most accurate, informative weekly newspaper possible while occasionally stirring a little healthy debate along the way. "Reagan told us we were the greatest nation in the world. It was packaged pride, probably the closest we've come in a while to that old sense of confidence," said Mason, whose observations had nothing to do with party politics. "But we have to deal in reality. As parents. As citizens. As people. We all know that the only way you really get back on top is by breaking your ass and doing it a piece at a time."

The feeling of America as a shining city on a hill, the images that Ronald Reagan projected, were heartwarming and perhaps even necessary after what had seemed to many a relentless, disillusioning string of losses: the assassinations of the Kennedy brothers and the Rev. Martin Luther King Jr., the televised unfolding of Vietnam, college protests and inner-city riots, the revelations of Watergate and subsequent Nixon resignation, the frustrations of gas shortages and stagflation and economic downsizing, the humiliation of hostages held month after month in Iran and the seeming impotence of Jimmy Carter's administration amidst it all. Young people had moved far from home in search of jobs; the old roles men and women had played were being redefined; the large numbers of working mothers and high rates of divorce were reshaping family life. Increasingly, the only thing that people seemed to share was contempt for Washington lobbyists, politicians and the commentators assessing it all. It felt good to be told we were good. Who couldn't use a comforting pat on the back? But looking out at the legacy of the last dozen years, it has grown harder and harder to embrace the vision.

"Every time a great reform has occurred in history, it's been after a tremendous crisis. Well, that's what we've got. Coming out of the economic and social wreckage, we have to ask ourselves: Are we going to roll up our sleeves?" Mason said, finishing his hamburger. "There are a lot of followers out there, but not a lot of doers. When you get down to it, though, it's up to you—up to us—to effect change. You. Me. All of us.

"You can't get it done all at once," he said. "And you can't get it done alone."

From tiny St. Marys in West Virginia to the heart of Los Angeles, in crowded city diners and ragged southern squares, at backyard barbecues and state fair exhibitions, citizens have told me the gig is up. Things, people say, have got to change. "We've reached a point where the economy, the violence, the state of our schools and questions about morality touch us all," Krieg said before heading off to meet with a student's parents.

"The question that America needs to ask itself isn't: 'What should I do?' We already know what needs to be done," he said. "The question is: 'What's keeping me from doing it?'"

• • •

Craning my neck to read the address on her shotgun-style home, I'd come to call on a regal woman of "a certain age" known to everyone around New Orleans simply as Miss Rose. The drapes were still drawn in the retired school teacher's meticulous living room, where framed photos of young relatives smiled out from atop the piano, the coffee table, the fireplace mantel—all of which were freshly dusted. This once had been, she said, a far grander neighborhood, a place with an entirely different feel. Within about an hour of my arrival that early morning, a shooting had occurred. "People talk all the time now about their rights, but really people have no regard for each other's rights. So what do you expect?"

She offered me coffee, then took a seat in a straight-backed chair. "Kids kill for name brands, for sneakers or what have you," she nearly spat, in a most genteel sort of way. "And those people on TV! I watch what they say and I can't believe that they're happy. Not too long ago, I think it was on *Oprah*, there were these couples who were into this—uh, what do they call it—swinging? It seems to me people go so far to find happiness. It's out of hand. Self indulgent people, that's what we've become.... We live in a society today where people feel, 'If I want it, I'll get it. And it doesn't matter how.' I'm close to a lot of the young people at church. And I tell them: 'Happiness isn't asking, expecting, grabbing. It's having faith.... Go back to the Bible.'"

Go back to the Bible. She would repeat these words a lot. They were words, I knew, that would draw mostly scoffs from street-calloused neighbors whose lives she said were wasted by "sin." But the next day I attended church with Miss Rose and felt sorry for the skeptics, the weary bunches scattered around, lazing up against cars with oversized beers in the morning and nothing much to do with the rest of the day. The alternative didn't seem very complicated: Give. Engage. Have faith. Change things.

In this noisy world, though, the sound of comfort is harder and harder to hear, too often drowned out by cursing, angry voices, poverty, addiction, self-loathing, the echo of gunfire down the street.

But listen closer. Then listen closer still.

There are voices like those raised each Sunday at New Zion Baptist Church just down the block from St. Charles Avenue. The imposing, boxy red-brick church is a fortress, a proud symbol of the hope and community that exists amidst the run-down blocks just away from the city's grand Garden District homes.

"Two are better than one," intoned the Rev. K. Alfred Sloane, a principal lector the morning I visited. God at your side gives strength. Loved ones by your side give strength. Reach out, he said. Reach farther. Do not walk alone.

"Because," the Rev. Sloane said again, "two are better than one."

Miss Rose had shed her plaid housedress in favor of a dark, conservative suit. Gap-toothed children in yellow ribbons scrambled here and there. The women of the Benevolent Society were all in white: white hats, white dresses, white gloves. The men wore coats and ties. They were mostly older men, some of whose sons were hanging out at the nearby strip mall, or in jail.

The congregation rose to sing, swaying together under the enormous whirring ceiling fans, voices rising and growing louder. Outside were racism and recession, children without fathers, drugs, despair.

But here, two were better than one.

"Faith is such a personal thing," Miss Rose had said earlier. "It's not something you can see or touch. I wouldn't dare tell you that I don't get upset or shed tears sometimes. I don't do everything that He would want me to do. But when I look out, I see people somehow not really trying at all. . . . There are ideals and principles that we all must follow. Without them, what are we?"

She had never married, had never really wanted to. She had kept to a small corner of the world, devotedly meting out equal measures of discipline to her students and to herself. Often, she said, she awakened hours before dawn to meditate and pray. "People get so lonely today," she said. "People don't know where to go." I imagined that in those early-morning hours she found something like peace. It wasn't an easy peace. She was a woman of limited means and witness to a steady stream of sadness, mute desperation in a neighborhood that had once worn more of a shine.

*Eloise Rose stands with her hymnal at the
New Zion Baptist Church in New Orleans.*

But she was a woman who carried herself with enormous dignity, speaking in a deep, steady cadence. She did not speak loudly, and each admonition she issued was followed by the caveat that she was far from perfect herself, that she had a long way to go. Why, I wondered, weren't more of us joined in her modesty?

"Sometimes I wonder," Miss Rose said the last time we spoke, "what is it that makes us hide inside, in a kind of closet all by ourselves? Why is it that we make the easy way hard, take the hard way and think it's easy? Maybe I didn't know any better, but I was happy coming up," she said shortly before reaching her eightieth birthday.

"We didn't have a lot—I don't mean that we didn't have food or decent clothes to wear—but we didn't have much. And somehow we were happy. We had a sense of pride and took comfort in knowing that there were things in the world, oh, not big and important things, but things that gave real nourishment, that made us feel we were not alone. It was pretty simple, I guess. We were a family."

She did not have all the answers. In fact, she had only a few. But of this much she was sure:

"Two are better than one."

Getting Together 6

Maturity Is about Daring to Make Change

There are so many stories to tell about people who have found new ways, better ways to stride forward together. They have put down roots wherever they are, whatever their circumstances, and set about making positive things grow. There is nothing wildly new in the impulse to foster home and community. Ronald Reagan spoke a decade ago of his hopes for a new "Morning in America" and three decades ago, John F. Kennedy asked us to ask what we could do for our country. But pretty words aren't enough at the end of the day.

At the end of the day, it's about respect—for yourself as well as for others—and genuine communication, not hyperbole, excuses and blame. The ground has been plowed and replowed, ruts and stones marked again and again. Is it possible that, like adolescents shaking off a long, moody sulk, we are gradually growing into the challenge, preparing to go out and start making necessary changes?

"People have felt baffled, frustrated and angry because the world that they used to have has gone. But they sense that there is an alternative, which they are enormously hungry to find," said author Robert Theobald, who has made the future of community a specialty. "I believe, as well as a growing number of other analysts and futurists, that the '90s are a cusp point in human history. We are either going to see things get a lot worse, or make them a lot better."

The battle belongs to the people, and it's the toughest kind. "Every government degenerates when trusted to the rulers of the people alone. The people themselves therefore are its only safe depositories," wrote Thomas Jefferson, so long ago. There is a sense of constant tension and anger and passion about this democratic enterprise that holds our future. I have heard a steady buzz among people who are ready to engage because, as all true adults know, beyond acts of God and nature, we alone ultimately are responsible for our fate.

You rear back. I just lost a job. My taxes aren't paid. My marriage is troubled, my kid out of control. Things are in too much of a mess. And anyway, what good can I do out there alone? But maybe being willing to stride out and stand up-front is part of the deal. Grow up! Maybe if you inch out into the fray, someone will be right there beside you. Maybe doing something more than complaining will actually feel good.

Well over a million volunteer and community service organizations exist in America today. Some 16 million citizens belong to 20,000 neighborhood crime watch programs. Hundreds of thousands of support groups for every kind of problem from joblessness to fear of flying gather regularly. Some $124 billion, most of it donated by individuals, goes to charity each year. Travel any distance on the nation's highways and you'll find long swaths adopted by citizens who keep them pruned and free of trash. On the sign welcoming you to just about any town, you'll find the logos of Kiwanis, Lions, Boys and Girls Clubs, the VFW, the 4H, synagogues and churches of every denomination. And from block to block, whether in the smallest hamlet or the largest urban hub, countless soup kitchens are run for the poor, Little Leagues for kids, hospices for the elderly, walkathons for the sick, bake sales for a local jungle gym, parades for hometown pride.

This chapter is full of citizens who have already made the leap. In ways big and small, they've started the ball rolling. They've put themselves on the line. They've grown up, taken some responsibility. How many of us can say the same?

• • •

I met Martha McCoy late one autumn at the Church of Christ Congregational in Newington, Connecticut, where she'd been invited to teach several dozen people from all walks of life how to start useful conversations in their hometowns. Conversations about race, about family, about jobs, about the environment, about what it might take to make their quality of life better. They were people who might have preferred a day puttering in the garden or watching a game on TV. They were minimum-wage workers and business leaders, politicians, pastors, educators, students and retirees, all preparing to gather in circles and listen to one another speak.

The Study Circles Resource Center, for which McCoy worked, found its wellspring in the 1991 Gulf War. As the long build-up of troops unfolded on TV, some 8,000 citizens requested handbooks designed to help them examine the intervention and issues it raised from a variety of angles. A simple softbound pamphlet, it offered no value judgments or particular assessment of America's response to Iraq's invasion of Kuwait. It merely offered basic information and a starting point for discussions among people who were confused—torn by wanting to support young servicemen and women but at the same time ambivalent about our reasons for having drawn a line in the sand. Since the war's end, a growing number of local groups have used similar Study Circles booklets on a range of difficult topics.

The session organized the Saturday I attended wasn't designed to push any particular agenda. There were no right or wrong answers, McCoy told me. And I knew she was right when I got to the sign-in desk and heard an older woman in a tight permanent hairdo turn to a younger man with an earring and say, "So, won't this be exciting?" Then, preempting any reply, she added, "Well, we might end up sounding like a bunch of old windbags. But I'll tell you this: At least we care." Her young friend smiled, and with that we all began trooping out of the church basement to a meeting room upstairs. A few people seemed to know each other, but mostly the participants sort of stood around near the door, looking as tentative as a bunch of kids on the first day of school. "Come on now," McCoy said, striding into the room. "Let's gather together. We've got lots of work to do."

First this one, then that began sliding metal-backed chairs into a misshapen circle. After some consideration, one woman with long, graying hair opted to sit on the floor. Breaking the silence with her engaging smile and gentle, yet no-nonsense manner, McCoy eased the group into the topic of the day: a discussion about why meaningful discussion seemed so hard to find.

"I'm not one who thinks of himself in terms of social activism, but in talking I realize I feel more strongly than I thought. I guess people are basically shy and unsure of themselves, nervous about sharing ideas," said a middle-aged man who looked profoundly uncomfortable.

"I think the resistance we feel about working together is often ignorance rather than a refusal to participate," a young woman added tentatively.

"It's concerns about how to open a dialogue without seeming too much like a 'social activist,'" the man continued, putting quotation marks around the term with his big, callused hands. "How do you avoid all those negative connotations?"

Somewhere along the line, the study circle participants agreed, getting involved and trying to make a difference had come to seem vaguely subversive or, maybe even worse, embarrassingly naive. The people gathered in this bare church classroom didn't want to be labeled or forced into anyone's narrow system of beliefs. They didn't want to heft a load of countercultural psycho baggage. And yet, much like so many other people across the country who gather in church basements and town halls, factory breakrooms and corner stores all the time, they wanted very much to act in socially conscious ways.

"People talk about the national debate. That phrase gets bandied about so much. But usually, it means that the media are talking about it," McCoy told me later. "In some ways, there aren't many safe spaces for people to come together and feel they own an issue. It belongs to somebody else—it belongs to Washington or journalists. You are just an observer."

People, she said, were slowly figuring out how to overcome this disconnected feeling because the risks in overlooking and continually excusing our nation's failings had grown too great. As many of her colleagues in other grassroots organizations had told me over the months, McCoy sensed a new energy afoot. She was encouraged by signs of a renewed interest in civic responsibility. And

I'd felt it too, watched citizens begin to engage in fresh and time-honored ways. It seemed this new energy was in large part pragmatic, a response stirred as much as anything by self-interest: more and more people share the sense that if the social tide doesn't begin to turn—and soon—even the strongest of swimmers would eventually be sucked out to sea.

I think that Americans have begun to realize that imprisoning young black men isn't just about breaking up families and eliminating potential contributors to society; it's also an enormous financial burden, one that taxpayers are finding harder and harder to carry. Political corruption isn't just the stuff of sarcastic late-night TV monologues; it undermines the faith of Americans and their willingness to participate in an enterprise that requires it. Sorry public education doesn't simply mean that those who can afford to will send their kids to private schools; it means that hundreds of thousands of other students entering an economy that increasingly depends on literacy and computer skills will be ill-prepared and unable to get jobs. And what's more, it also means an ever-greater demand for welfare support from an ever-narrower base of working people. The steady decline of real wages, high rates of teen pregnancy and drug addiction, spread of AIDS and homelessness aren't just problems that belong to some distant city or town. They cost us all in dollars and in lives. And how high will be the price paid by generations of children now growing up without dreams, without a sense of purpose or passion? They are inner-city kids, surely, but they are also kids from "good" suburban homes. Some carry guns and belong to gangs and show up in the headlines. Many, many others are simply walking gape-mouthed through endless, airless malls in search of something to do.

"The opportunity I see within communities is to have

a real dialogue and make everyone a player in the future," said Benjamin Dixon, an eloquent deputy education commissioner for the state of Connecticut who joined the group at the Church of Christ Congregational the day Martha McCoy visited. "The degree to which you can get people together, you can get people out of isolation and begin to see the connecting points—the connecting points between personal, individual needs and the community's needs. In the past we've walked away from the public table, had our conversations one-on-one in the dark. Now we have a chance to put these issues on the public table.... When you compare now with the '70s and '80s, people are more prepared [to participate]. But it's not necessarily a conscious thing yet. People know something has to change. Our challenge is to find the hook, draw everyone into turning things around."

At the end of the session, over brown-bag lunches, the study circle spread out around a table to watch a videotape about Lima, Ohio, a town whose citizens used a Study Circles guide to confront a spectrum of issues related to race. Meeting in small groups over coffee in each other's living rooms, men and women of all ages and backgrounds had exchanged tough questions and frank opinions about their perceptions and misperceptions, their hopes and concerns with regard to one another and the future of their midwestern town. No monumental changes were engineered. No court or commission was at their backs. It was simply one person to another, citizens working things out.

"It's kind of like alcoholism. Before you can start making things better, you first have to admit that you've got a problem," said a young man interviewed for the video. "Blame is useless at this point," he said.

Looking around, I saw several people nod as the

screen went to black. Someone got up from the table now strewn with apple cores and half-eaten sandwiches. And all at once, with the flip of a switch, the overhead lights had come on.

• • •

Part of being an adult, the meaning of maturity, is understanding that dreams don't always work out, that disappointment crops up again and again. It means accepting but not being overwhelmed by these immovable facts. It means defying ready bitterness, denying frustration and anger the berths that they constantly seek. It means moving on, trying again.

For the guy who sees job prospects as limited by his white-male status, it means sending out more resumes. For the teacher whose students defy discipline, it means trying new methods. For the successful entrepreneur whose stomach turns at the mention of taxes, welfare or crime, it means putting on a pair of jeans and seeing to it that his dollars are at work. For the religious, it means practicing tolerance. For the victims of discrimination, it means redoubling efforts to educate those who would hate them. For the vast many who find no single focus, but nonetheless feel disenfranchised, alienated, limited, it means embracing the chaos, then doing something different.

Otherwise, it stands to reason, we will only get more of the same.

These are basic tools of adulthood, tools a group of young people I met in Newark, New Jersey, had already begun to grasp. They had excuses, ample reasons for doing all the wrong things, for copping all kinds of pleas. Instead they were among the first to initiate a program called Do Something.

Getting a Life   *137*

Gathered quietly in an unremarkable room, their backpacks and winter parkas jumbled among folding chairs, the young group was at work writing their obituaries the night that I visited.

Brenda Sanchez, twenty-four, was "a great achiever."

Todd Behling, twenty-five, "worked and achieved at everything he put his mind to, and his love of humanity defined his chosen work."

Hoover Herrera, twenty-three, would "be best remembered as a man who liked to do anything to make someone else's life a little happier. To his family, he'll be remembered as a strong and responsible father who never put his needs above anyone else's in his home. To his community, which was the city of Newark, he will be remembered for his concerns and efforts in helping youth by providing many positive opportunities for them to take advantage of."

Jill Rottman, twenty-one, would "be remembered most for her focus on the successful revamping of the welfare system, which eventually brought the program to an end. [This drew big applause.] She was also responsible for initiating housing programs that provided homes to millions of Americans who would not have had them otherwise. Most importantly, however, she started a program that rid the country of the illegal drugs that used to plague our cities."

John Hill, the twenty-year-old whose job it was to lead the night's discussion, stopped the exercise. Though the group had been asked to start with their endings, his talk was actually about new beginnings. He and his young colleagues were there to seize possibility, he said, and commit themselves to the kind of vision these future dreams would require.

"Right now, everyone in here has done an obituary," said Hill, a New Jersey Youth Corps counselor by day. "So if you have that in mind every day of your life, or every day when you wake up, *everything* you do should *reflect* where you want to be at in the end. You understand that?"

Everyone nodded. It was pretty basic stuff, as basic as their group's name. The brainchild of twenty-something *Melrose Place* actor Andrew Shue and his childhood buddy, Michael Sanchez, the goals envisioned for Do Something were simple: to give the nation's younger citizens—a group often scorned or overlooked—the chance to make a difference. The fund, which was officially launched in May 1994, administered grants of up to $500 to innovators under the age of thirty, young people who might want to start a hospice or day care center for single mothers, tutor peers or help build affordable housing. The field was wide open, the only requirement being that proposals be creative and practical.

Even though it was getting late and getting home would be troublesome on this frigid night, a certain quiet energy moved around the circle of chairs, among the multicolored group of bright, young people whose idealism many in America have defined as dead.

It is impossible to know for sure how engaged or disaffected young people as a whole are today. Finding high school dropouts and apathetic mall rats is easy, but fierce strivers are also out there to be found. Teen mothers and pubescent criminals make headlines, but peer counselors and student leaders and morally responsible kids are out there in abundance as well.

"Young people have a whole bunch of energy, enthusiasm, idealism and almost invariably want to take action," said Sanchez, twenty-six, director of Do Something's main office in New York. "But there are few resources and structures in place. Our local boards can combine all this energy with a little bit of money and a lot of guidance. . . .

It has to happen on the local level. And young people know their communities."

By enlisting the help of seasoned community activists who might act as mentors, Do Something had moved to establish autonomous boards of young directors to administer funds in a half-dozen cities. Ultimately, the hope was that these partnerships would spread and thrive nationwide. Thanks in part to Shue's star connections, the fledgling organization had received celebrity support and commitments of airtime from Fox Broadcasting and MTV. Several major magazines had made free ad space available and Blockbuster Video had agreed to make the group's materials available at hundreds of outlets.

The whole enterprise may or may not take off. Only time will tell. But at least, said Greg Tighe, one of the young supporters present in Newark that night, "it's an idea, a plan to 'Do Something' before you die, to try making a real difference in the world . . . to leave something positive behind in an environment that right now seems just focused on the negative."

Outside the brick building on Martin Luther King Jr. Boulevard, planes were slowly descending one after the other from flight patterns into Newark Airport. The icy streets were mainly empty, though area police later told me they would log 2,187 crime reports over the next twenty-four hours. Inside and upstairs, over Chinese take-out and steady rounds of applause, were young people beating the odds. Many had lost siblings or friends to the streets; many had known temptation themselves.

Jermaine Puryear, a recent grant recipient, had been standing squarely in trouble's path not so long ago. His mother had been into drugs and his father "wasn't really there for me." By the time he was sixteen, his high school career was over and a baby soon would be born.

Carjacking, which made its name in Newark, was the crime of choice among many of the young man's neighborhood friends. I couldn't help but think of Jessie Johnson, see shades of Paducah.

Puryear hadn't gotten into any serious trouble with the law, "but I could see it coming." Fortunately, some good people showed up along the way. At a local church and in community groups, he found mentors and spiritual guides who intervened to set him on another path, a path that since has only widened. With help from Do Something and a grant from President Clinton's new Corporation for National Service, Puryear had started a program that would combine auto body repair and high school equivalency courses with life lessons, support and a strong emphasis on self-discipline. Teenagers who might otherwise have been penned in overcrowded juvenile detention centers would instead have the chance to work off probationary community service by learning how to repair cars, something they could actually use in a socially responsible way. "You know, a lot of these guys can get into a car in thirty seconds," said Puryear, who had seen it done plenty of times. "You might have a genius on your hands—a real rocket scientist. Why not give them a second chance?"

Nailha Williams, a nineteen-year-old Do Something board member who had a few months earlier given birth to her second child saw things in much the same way. "All you see is negativity—especially in the city of Newark. And that gets to you after a while," she said, giving one of those "negative" reporters a tentative smile. She said she'd felt lost, felt very alone until an older friend stepped in to point out a different way, helping to put her in contact with the group she stood with that night.

"What I've learned is that you can make a difference,"

she said. "A lot of people don't think they can. I didn't think I could."

But she had, and the difference she was making was not necessarily small.

• • •

Debra Hoeft was not so long ago a woman who felt alone and incapable. I can't remember anymore exactly how we came to meet. But the story I eventually wrote was about her life with a boy named Eric, a child born with Down syndrome, who introduced his family to a world that would never again be the same.

"You hope to have perfect kids. You expect it. So I was devastated, of course," said Mrs. Hoeft, who made her home in the Long Island town of Patchogue, New York. "But this was my child. I wasn't going to abandon him just because he wasn't perfect. Just because it wasn't easy."

Soon after Eric was born, a social worker had floated into Debra Hoeft's hospital room like a life raft. Here is someone who can help me help my son, the new mother thought. Here is someone who understands. She brightened until the social worker asked, "So, Mrs. Hoeft, are you going to keep him?"

Mrs. Hoeft wasn't an extraordinary woman. But she knew that no matter what it took, she would find a way to give this child whose problems were foreign to her the best opportunities he could possibly receive. It was not a simple determination. Sure, the maternal impulse to protect her child was there. The isolation, though, nearly snuffed it out.

When Eric was born, Mrs. Hoeft was totally unprepared. Though 80 percent of some 5,000 Down syndrome babies are born each year to women under thirty-five, she had believed herself exempt from risk. She and her husband had no reason to suspect this child would run any slower or dream any smaller than their other three high-spirited sons. The pregnancy had been normal, the mother in her twenties and healthy, the delivery smooth. But Eric was born with an extra chromosome, a single blip on the genetic map that would reshape his life, and the life of his family.

Mrs. Hoeft sensed something was wrong the first time she held him. His tongue appeared oversized, his eyes mildly slanted. "But what did I know about it?" she said much later.

Debra and Peter Hoeft had no idea how much they would have to teach this child, or how well he would show them how to learn. They had never really thought about retardation at all, except to silently count their blessings. "Thank God ours are healthy. Thank God our children are 'normal.'"

Then God or the fates or whatever label you might choose dealt them a different hand. "I felt sorry for Eric because I knew things would never be easy," said Peter, a stocky firefighter. He wept like a child when he learned this son would never be like the other kids, then joined his wife in confronting a different future. For Debra, the sight of healthy, pink babies in the maternity ward was almost too much to bear. When a nurse sent her home with the standard package of complimentary magazines for new parents, it seemed a bitter joke. "All I could think was, 'Why are they giving me these? These magazines have nothing to do with my new baby.'"

No one came to explain what Down syndrome would mean. Nobody told her how to care for this child, what kinds of programs were out there for him. There were no signs pointing the way to help. And so it was up to the Hoefts to grope their way from isolation toward a web of support.

"Not long after Eric was born, I saw a girl—a girl with Down syndrome—standing on a street corner with her mother. And I just grabbed that mother's sleeve, held on and began crying. She was the first person I'd met who knew what I was going through," said Mrs. Hoeft. "For the first time since Eric was born, I wasn't alone."

By the time her eyes were dried, Debra Hoeft had found an invaluable friend and adviser in JoAnn Vindigni. Finally, that much-needed life raft had arrived.

The Hoefts soon connected to a whole network they'd had no idea existed. They joined local support groups, contacted national associations and tracked down literature that would shape the course they took with Eric. But they also did something more. In all their confusion and anguish, Peter and Debra Hoeft found ways to touch and be touched.

They set about starting a magazine for parents like themselves, a practical compendium that would offer help as well as humor in dealing with what they'd come to see as no more than an unexpected challenge in their lives. Based out of their ranch-style home about two hours outside of New York City, the Hoefts established a cottage-style operation funded largely with credit card advances the couple could ill-afford. Soon after they came up with idea of publishing a magazine, they found a spontaneous support system of writers, artists and all-around boosters. People like the Vindigni family and the guy down at the local copy shop, who as it turned out had a sister with Down syndrome and was happy to contribute free typesetting. Chris Burke, a teenager with Down syndrome who starred in *Life Goes On*, a now-defunct TV series, had some time to spare for a cover story. A bookstore chain executive whose daughter had Down syndrome offered to help with distribution. And so it went.

Peter and Debra Hoeft weren't natural-born crusaders. All he ever wanted was a city job and steady paycheck. All she truly craved was a couple of kids. But Eric changed all that. He drew the Hoefts into fellowship with some 250,000 families touched by Down syndrome. He brought them new friends and a commitment to helping people who otherwise would feel alone. Confronted with a child who had limitations, they reached beyond their fear.

Out there, stitched into the fabric of America, are all sorts of people who don't know all the answers but have found tens of thousands of good starts. In Columbia, South Carolina, federal and local funds have been used to provide low-interest loans to police officers who buy homes in low-income neighborhoods, a program that has been a model for other cities around the nation. In Santa Monica, California, a computer bulletin board once available only to private subscribers now provides community access to recreational classes, public documents, job opportunities, a consumer complaint center, pet adoption, recycling rules, cultural events and city council agendas through twenty-five public terminals in various seniors centers, libraries and schools. A program to help the homeless grew out of on-line discussions among citizens who were strangers. On New York's Long Island, a man similarly concerned with those being left off the computer superhighway devised a plan through which companies can donate machines that might otherwise be junked and invited beginners to take volunteer-led classes from which they would eventually graduate, taking their new, used computers home. In Los Angeles, former gang members have united to help battle wildfires. In Fort Wayne, Indiana, housewives and assorted "little people" have blocked a hazardous waste site's proposed expansion. At the ABC Television Network, executives have committed to a public service campaign that brought children's issues into millions of U.S. homes. In Chicago, a businessman who didn't think owning a car had to be a prerequisite to life started a van service to shuttle inner-city workers out to corporate compounds in the suburbs.

There is more. So much more. More good news than any newspaper could publish, more action than any blue-ribbon panel or Washington commission could begin to conceive. In commuter suburbs, neighbors who once passed each other in cars are hosting discussion groups and salons. In urban areas long victimized by crime and drugs, more and more citizens have reclaimed their streets. Towns in recession have worked around setbacks, adjusted to economic changes. Everywhere, all kinds of people have found ways to fight back.

But how do you, the guy running a creative educational program, know that she, a woman down the street, started something similar in her last hometown? How do they, a group of stressed-out mothers who want to found a day care center, link up with them, a group of senior citizens one town over who have love and energy to spare? How do we know we're not alone when our doors are closed, our town squares so shut down? How do we find ways to understand each other's cultures, histories, differing points of view when so many of us give up for feeling there is no one to talk with, no one to hear?

The Hoefts had no choice but to find new ways of listening. They had learned how to help Eric practice the speech, physical and occupational techniques prescribed by the cavalcade of therapists who visited their home each week. They had watched his three brothers, all under fourteen years old, learn to be tireless playmates, protectors and friends. "It's a big thing for most parents when a child takes a first step. For us, it's if he sits up or reaches for something," said Peter Hoeft, who had found places in his heart that he'd never before known existed.

"As he grows up, if he wants to play baseball, he'll play baseball. If he wants to join Cub Scouts, he can do that," said Mr. Hoeft. "But he's also got to learn there will be certain things he cannot do."

Eric would never head a corporation or command an army. Like all but the rarest males with Down syndrome, he surely would be sterile. He would never drive a car or make first-string. But with all those limitations, Debra and Peter Hoeft only found more options—both for their child's life, and for their own. They refused to be intimidated. They refused to be made insecure—not about themselves or about the life their Down syndrome baby might live.

"Let's face it," Mr. Hoeft said, "Eric will always be different. He'll never be a cop or a fireman. But he can be a whole lot of other things. He can be happy."

"Happy," Mrs. Hoeft repeated the last time we spoke. "That's what all of us want to be. But in all the fear I've felt with Eric, I've learned something else. I've learned that a lot of times we're just running away. Running from fear, running from insecurity and shame. That's what makes—or destroys—life. The feeling that maybe you are something, well, something less than what you could actually be."

• • •

Sometimes where we least expect it, we find the greatest sustenance and hope. For me, when I think of the gay community, I think of Rob Parker. And when I think of Rob Parker, I am reminded of the amazing fortune sometimes found in unlikely places. A mutual acquaintance introduced us when I needed some real estate help. "This guy is great," my friend said. "He'll steer you the right way." It was unspoken, but I had a hunch this mutual acquaintance of ours was making a coy attempt at a match. Two single people, maybe there would be a spark. I liked Rob immediately and I think he liked me. We sometimes met for late-night dinners after work or lunch on the fly. On occasion he brought me to business-related functions. It was all very nice. But something was a little awry. This guy is terrific, I thought to myself. Attractive, successful, astute, funny and kind. So how come no spark? It just wasn't there. The months went along, this piece still askew, when one morning at my newly purchased apartment, over omelets and toast, I got to talking about some personal, mildly revealing things.

"OK. Now I feel really awkward. You have to share something personal with me," I said to Rob, who put down his fork and paused only briefly, though it seemed a long while.

"OK," he said. "Well, I live with someone..."

The cad, I thought to myself. He's here secretly at breakfast with me while his girlfriend is dozing at home. No doubt he's got a sad story about how they've been having problems for quite some time.

"... and his name is Peter."

I would pay for a picture of the stunned look on my face. But in the awkward moments that followed, as I scrambled to regain some politically correct composure, I think our friendship began. We laughed and cried that morning, the big block finally moved out of place. Rob and Peter are two amazing men whom I would never have known had it not been for a misguided match-making acquaintance who thought he'd found me a true love.

And, in a way, he had.

In the summer of 1981, the bit of land outside New York harbor called Fire Island was ablaze, drugs and sex in abundant supply. Some had seen the *New York Times* article about an illness described as "gay cancer." Some had friends who were mysteriously sick, but not many. Some had heard rumblings about possible links between these illnesses and sexual promiscuity, but infrequently. Some felt panicky twinges, but remained in good health. This would pass, they told themselves.

They would be fine.

Of course, we now know much more of the story. Well over a million Americans—of all ages, sexual orientations and backgrounds—are HIV-infected. Hundreds of thousands of men, women and children have died. On its deadly way, this virus has brought out the best and worst in people. After writing an article on AIDS some months ago, I received a letter from a man who seemed reasonable but said he had no compassion when it came to the disease, taking exception with my suggestion that it had made "extraordinary heroes" of some "ordinary people."

My words weren't meant to glorify the gay community or to endorse any political or moral agenda. All I meant to say was that if heroism could be defined as acting with courage and nobility, then many had done so—often overcoming personal reservations and fears in order simply to care for the sick and dying. But because AIDS has been most closely identified with a particular group whose "lifestyle," for lack of a better word, many find repugnant, it has naturally been about more than suffering. It has also been about secrets and virulent fear.

And so, I ask those who find no patience with this disease to suspend judgment for a moment. Because this passage might be relevant to any number of groups, whatever their political or philosophical or religious persuasion. The kind of commitment that pastors and politicians, parents and teachers call for again and again with little success has been wrenched from the gay community. From the most adverse possible circumstances, a lifesaving if brutal crossbreed of compassion and honesty and purpose has emerged.

For all the exuberant excess alive the summer that AIDS appeared on the horizon, there was also a sense of emptiness in the abandon. "It was sexual Camelot," a gay man who eventually joined the ranks of activists once told me. "We really felt that the world was our oyster. The worst you had were sexually transmitted diseases, which were looked on as a temporary inconvenience. It was all part of the climate. There was an unexamined quality to it."

The AIDS plague, for all its merciless death, has also played midwife to a new kind of life. It has summoned great unity and purpose from a community that had been operating on pretty much an every-man-for-himself basis. "Now my life is about going to the hospital and seeing how this one is doing, whether that one has food, if my lover is OK," the activist continued. "I feel not like I'm forty-five, but that I'm sixty-five. It's inconceivable the totality with which it touches you. I mean, I wasn't prepared for this. None of us were."

The gay community, whatever the moral disdain you might feel, was functioning on a level not so different from the kind we all function on. They were seeking pleasure, not particularly concerned with sacrifice or service or self-denial. This was *their* turn, and they were taking it for all they could. It took wide-scale tragedy, the loss of friend after friend after friend, to bring a whole new perspective, a new sort of sobriety and commitment to life. At first it was a question of addressing immediate, obvious concerns: Hospital workers afraid of infection were leaving dinner trays by bedridden patients' doors. Social Security workers were ducking appointments with the afflicted. Men needed their diapers changed, grocery shopping done, wills drawn, hands held through the most terrifying moments.

As time wore on, and the list of dead and dying grew ever longer, the challenge went further. Research funds had to be raised and politicians lobbied; the media had to be educated as did the many heterosexuals, teenagers, IV drug-users and spouses who might not realize they too were at risk. Hospices were founded, newsletters were produced. Mothers, fathers, teachers, ministers, co-workers, men and women of all sexual orientations and political persuasions found that they would not be untouched. Death's bony finger tapped at more and more backs.

Out on the Great Lawn in Central Park late one spring, 30,000 people who defied all stereotypes gathered for an annual AIDS walk. Rob and Peter and I wandered among the crowd as songs were sung and, in speeches and silence, the dead were mourned. Balloons floated up into a clear blue sky and, as different as everyone was, we all streamed out of the park to walk mile after mile together. It was bittersweet to find so much focus and energy, so many commitments and connections that, but for the specter of ongoing loss, might never have been made.

Shortly before the gathering, I'd interviewed Dr. Larry Mass, one of the founders of the Gay Men's Health Crisis, which had become a model for future caring organizations of all kinds. He said he'd recently seen a flier publicizing the upcoming AIDS walk posted at the local YMCA where he'd exercised regularly since shortly after arriving in New York back in 1979. As he paused before the announcement, years suddenly slipped away, the loss of friends and weight of fear ebbing momentarily. What he saw instead was something extraordinary. "It was astounding," the soft-spoken doctor said. "I felt this tremendous pride and sense of real progress. [The gay community] could never have come this far without this horrible epidemic. All of our issues and needs and all of the confrontation has happened because of AIDS.

"So, am I tired? Am I tired? Yes," said Mass, forty-eight, a private person who had been a somewhat reluctant leader. "But it's a good kind of tired. The only way to conceptualize it is as a war. Think of us like Beirut or Sarajevo, where every day you're hearing of deaths, deaths of friends. It's cost so much. We're numb, completely numb at times.

"But," he said. "we have fought together, which means something."

Out of the loss, a community of people had grown where once only a large group of individuals had existed. The aimless cruising and one-night stands had for many been replaced with life-and-death bonds. Drug abuse and political insouciance, escapism and irresponsibility had diminished. In their place a network based in friendship and common purpose had flourished; life-saving bridges had been built. Many believe that under different circumstances, absent the tremendous stress of AIDS, they are bridges that might otherwise have been burned.

There is no moral to the story. Too many people have died for that.

"But there is still something there. Where there once was a lot of hedonism and total self-interest, there now is a community, a real sense of unity and connection," explained my friend Rob, whose younger generation came of age after AIDS had already transformed the view. "It has forced us to grow up in some ways. And in some ways, that's not such a bad thing. Painful, yes. Horrifying, absolutely. But not entirely bad."

• • •

Meet the people of Steelville, Missouri. Take a look at what they made once they decided to make something together. Theirs is the story of a nucleus of citizens who bridged the distance between slow death and a life full of possibility. Theirs is a story of commitment, hard work, ingenuity and caring.

Most of all, it's about hope.

In 1990, the Census Bureau placed Steelville, Missouri, and its 1,470 citizens at the geographic center of the nation's drifting population. That small accident, which came with a commemorative plaque, provided a nice little psychological boost, but mostly just got in the way when the town lawn had to be mowed. This claim to fame wouldn't bring the town back.

And so the renaissance had to find its steam elsewhere, in the town itself. "It's up by our own bootstraps," said John Britton, owner of the local funeral parlor. "We sensed we were dying—and that no one was going to salvage us. We had to do it ourselves," added Ike Lovan, who ran a jewelry shop and rooming house known as the White Eagle.

About an hour south of St. Louis, the town had lost commerce and jobs to malls and factories nearby but not close enough. Still, they had some basic raw materials—a local newspaper, a shoe factory, a small machine tool company, a county courthouse, several active churches and the Meramec River which, along with a ring of wooded hills, was something of a tourist draw. These things, they determined, were good enough to build something better upon. "We're on the western frontier of the Ozarks,"

Lovan said of his hometown, which stretched about a mile and a half from east to west. "Like the pioneers, we're making our way. We see something out there, and we're using our resources and people to get there."

A big key to Steelville's success was the local telephone company, a cooperative that citizen shareholders for their own quirky reasons had always maintained independently. It was in many ways this bit of historical whimsy that gave the town its first break, or at least the chance to make their own good luck. It had started a few years back with a gamble: The telephone company's citizen-run board risked $5,000 to buy a shot at a federal lottery for regional cellular phone rights—and won. Quickly reselling their license to a larger communications company netted a tidy profit of several million dollars. A large chunk of that windfall was plowed immediately into a community development corporation, which since has provided seed money for a number of public projects.

For starters, the town invested in state-of-the-art telephone technology, not too common in rural areas. The thinking was that it would be a bargaining chip, something to offer prospective businesses in addition to enterprise-zone incentives like tax breaks and free property. With a telecommunications system sophisticated enough to compete with those in many major cities, Steelville would be a viable alternative for companies looking to relocate. Building on that idea, town leaders figured that good housing at affordable prices could only make the deal that much more appealing. So they set to work, designing a family-friendly housing development that might also attract retirees with disposable income. It didn't hurt, either, that with each new resident there would come a new phone installation, a steady boost both for the phone company and the overall local economy.

Such enterprises, and the pooling of local resources, have driven Steelville's best efforts. Citizens got together to clean up Yadkin Creek, landscaping its banks and stocking it with trout that now drew vacationers. The Brown Shoe factory might have been among others that were shut down elsewhere when the company scaled back, but a corporate executive born in Steelville lobbied and at least delayed its demise and the loss of several hundred jobs. A dentist who dreamed of having a country music show found a consortium of local investors interested in buying an eyesore-of-an-abandoned car dealership. It was now a motel with a 400-seat auditorium that drew steady summertime crowds. A coalition of churches had gotten together to run a food pantry for those fallen on tough times. Another group convinced Burlington Northern Railroad to donate a vintage caboose the town could use as an information bureau and jungle gym. Technology buffs got involved with installing an interactive video resource center so citizens could tune in classes at any Missouri state university or browse through the Library of Congress.

"In some ways, this community is a model of what this country was like years ago: Life is on an intimate scale," said the Rev. William Guyer Birch, co-pastor with his wife at the local Presbyterian church. "You still have here everything you have in a city—crime, drugs, domestic troubles. The difference is people here have taken the initiative. There are plenty of communities nearby where grass is growing up between the crumbling, abandoned stores. People knew things were changing. And they asked the important question: What are we changing to? Change is threatening. But we all still have to ask ourselves: What kind of people are we becoming?"

The most obvious answer was perhaps to be found on

Main Street itself, where the newly refurbished shops all seemed to be named for someone: Al's Cafe, Bill's General Store, Sherry's Flowers, Nancy's Antiques. The whole strip shimmered, in a low-key way. A few years ago, locals told me, you wouldn't have found much. But that was another story.

Main Street's revival had started several years before with a town dinner at the Golden Echoes retirement home, which in itself embodied the town's entrepreneurial flair. Constructed with local money, the center included a reception hall where residents catered events, using the profits to subsidize senior meals. No federal funds for this group, early planners declared. They would instead find ways to generate their own income and contribute to the community as well.

So at this dinner a few years back, fancy hors d'oeuvres were served with wines from local vineyards. Merchants were shown an architect's plans for returning Main Street to its historical roots. A local banker offered $500,000 of loans at 5 percent—half the going rate—to anyone who joined in the renewal effort. Nineteen shop owners immediately signed on, and the number soon doubled. "Everybody wants to be part of something positive," said Ed Leonard, a relative newcomer who had started a graphics business in town. "Five years ago, things here were desolate, abandoned. But we started out with a few people and watched most of the community join in."

Of course, there were those who objected. There were those who saw a self-interested cabal of self-styled community leaders out only for themselves. It took just the briefest visit to the West End Tavern, a dark place whose heavy oak bar was not without its charms, to find people who were disgruntled. But you had to wonder what good they thought their moaning would do in a town with limited options. A vocal group of naysayers had opposed plans to build a new town pool to replace the decrepit one built back in 1953, despite the fact that an early poll found 85 percent of citizens said it was something they wanted. "Spend a half-million on a swimming pool? For who? Who's going to pay for it?" said one fellow, pretty much summing up the opposition feeling. When the ballot came up, the group lobbying against won a narrow victory. The pool was dead, supporters thought.

Until a local man who chose to remain anonymous stepped forward. He offered to match whatever money the community could raise during 1993. Progress was swift and carefully charted on posters around town. At a community auction, one family offered a home-cooked gourmet meal that sold for $150. A local innkeeper offered a free canoe ride and stay in one of his cabins, which fetched $200. And so it went. The town raised $15,000 in a single night, which was added to the proceeds from an antique doll show, bake sales and the like. By the end of the year, nearly $70,000 had been raised, bit by hard-earned bit.

"In this town, if you have a problem and ask a hundred people for help, eighty or ninety will stand up and pitch in, whether it's going to pick up rocks in the park or whatever," said Bob Bell, whose whole family was well known around town. One brother had been elected mayor. His dad had been a judge. They would qualify as big players, members of the informal aristocracies that, for better or worse, exist in and shape small communities and large around the nation. I'd gone up to meet him because several people around Steelville had said I could not miss this place called Wildwood Springs. Buying the old lodge had been a bit cockeyed, Bell admitted. But as he edged toward thirty, he'd heard a voice not unlike the one that inspired Kevin Costner's character in the movie *Field of Dreams*.

"If you restore it," the voice had said, "they will come."

Settled into one of his beloved old rocking chairs out on the lodge's wide back porch, Bell mused on what had kept a young guy with a college degree so close to home. He'd gone away to school but found himself drawn back, eventually taking over the management of a small manufacturing company and working on Wildwood, which he and several other family members had purchased from longtime friends ready to retire. It was something in his mind's eye, he said. "People of my generation, we all had these big expectations. We all wanted new homes—my Polos, my Dockers and all that good stuff. I made a whopping $7,000 my first year back in Steelville. All my friends went into slick jobs and bought new cars. . . . [But] not a one of them is still working for the same company and I don't think a one has done better." Many had been divorced. Many, the happily married father of two assessed, "thought if they weren't driving a BMW that something was wrong." Now, he said, many were wondering otherwise.

A train whistle blew in the distance while we quietly rocked, the spirit of Wildwood's 1920s splendor echoing all around us. You could almost hear the old big band sounds, see young couples swaying together, maybe doing a fox trot across the scuffed plank floors. And Bell said he could see something else. He could see future seasons, hear the laughter of families like his gathered around the big hearth, ambling down the rambling lawn.

Sunset was around the corner. Bell had had a long day

between work down at the factory and deciding which bedspreads would hold up best but still look nice in lodge seasons to come. His mother and father wandered over from their house across the street, Dad enjoying a cocktail, Mom offering her two-cents on changes through the decades around town. And we all rocked a while more, pondering the state of the union. What had kept the younger Bell and his brothers around Steelville?

It was home.

"We have a very strong 'Take care of yourself' attitude here," said Bell, who had made a hobby of studying his town's long history. "It's a family. And the neat thing is, there's more than one person pushing the buttons. We've got a community here and, to a lot of people, it's worth working for."

Getting a Life 7
Don't You Know It's Wherever You Are?

The night the Tommy Dorsey Orchestra left me, it broke my heart.

It wasn't intentional, of course. But that's the thing about heartbreak. It's often unintended.

They played the songs that America once fell in love to and, like a World War II veteran, I, too, quickly succumbed. It hit me like a bolt while we were out on the road, traveling from state to state in their rolling locker room of a bus. I'd gone along just to capture some of the smell and feel, write a little story about one of the last great big bands still playing out-of-the-way nightclubs and high school gyms in endless one-night stands. I wasn't looking for romance when I suggested the assignment. But from the first moment I saw the Dorsey Orchestra's leader Buddy Morrow's twinkly eyes and patrician crest of thick, white hair, I was a goner. As the French say, it was a *coup de foudre*. Thunder struck, and I was head-over-heels.

They do not know this, or at least so I think, but late at night I watched them sleep, scribbling away in my reporter's notebook as we drove on until dawn. I adore these musicians, I thought, glancing up and down their overstuffed bus, its aisle filled with a jumble of arms, legs, hands, feet. Though ours would be only a brief encounter, these exhausted men folded like pretzels into their seats unwittingly gave me all that I'd been searching for over so many years, through so many miles and weeks. Suddenly I was out on the road, overwhelmed by the sense of being in it together. Bumping happily along, I smiled to myself as we passed through darkened towns and slid among cornfields, dawn eventually coming into view. There was more than just me. There were these men and their radiant music, that indefinable swing.

They were seventeen guys from all walks of life, spanning ages twenty-four to seventy-five, a band of individual styles making great music together. Theirs was a big sound, the sound of what we now remember as a gentler time in America. Much of their repetoire was a half-century old. And yet somehow, perhaps because they breathed so much into it, everything they played was completely alive. Their music lifted rooms, revived flagging spirits. I saw men in their 70s reach back to slide an arm around women they'd loved since the days when love was forever and leaving meant going to war. And though there weren't many, I saw on young faces the look of discovery, like teenagers smitten with something as old as the ages, yet totally new. Buddy Morrow and his boys were a throwback, their music a remnant of a very different time. Perhaps a less cynical time, a less hurried time, a time not quite so angry. Theirs was a brassy sound, the sound of energy, their beat one that used to drive people into each other's arms and out onto the floor.

"I hear you're writing a story," an old man in Louisville, Kentucky, said to me, light in his eyes. "I don't know who you are, but save the music. Please don't let this music die."

When Buddy's trombone faded into "I'm Getting Sentimental over You" a short time later, I knew that the signature song was his way of saying goodnight. Louisville was the last stop I would make with the band. Just after 1 A.M. in an empty parking lot out behind the club where they'd just finished their gig, we milled about in the chill, misty air saying repeated good-byes. It was back up to Chicago tonight. They would be driving straight on until dawn. One by one, Buddy's boys got back on the bus. "You be good now," Tom Sapienza, a dear, sad-eyed piano player said, giving my trench coat's collar a tug. Then he, too, climbed aboard the bus. A few minutes later they'd driven off, leaving me behind.

It was only a few short blocks to my motel. I dragged my feet. Why this emptiness? Like a doctor, I'd always been surgical and precise. Though I'd cared for everyone I'd ever met, bled a little with each story I'd told, there had always been that neat separation. Like Icarus dropping into a scene, I'd remained at the corners, just at the edge of the frame. I'd committed the reporter's perfect crime time and again, binding other people's lives into neat little packages, then moving on.

I put the key in my motel room door, turned on a lamp. The place looked like so many I'd slept in before. So many nights all at once were a blur. Maybe because by now tears brimmed in my eyes, began to spill down my cheeks. Still wearing my trench coat and pumps, I fell into a lump on the bed. "What is wrong with you?" I kept asking myself. But the sobbing would not stop. I was having the cry of my life, and even now I'm not exactly sure why.

It just somehow seemed that everyone I'd ever loved,

all the people I'd ever met, every friend I'd ever known was on the bus with the Dorsey Orchestra as it drove off into the night.

I got up, washed my face and looked in the mirror. It was not an unfamiliar drill. But this time I paused for a long while, looking at my reflection, at the lines that had begun to settle around my mouth and at the corners of my eyes. I saw a very old woman. And then suddenly, I saw a young girl, an open heart, my best friend. I saw countless friends, precious encounters, all kinds of love and laughter and sadness and confusion welling up in my eyes. I'd not been so alone on the road. I'd just had a problem with seeing.

Growing up is about a lot of serious things. Harsh realities, tough decisions, trade-offs, defeats. But in all their messiness, the ridiculousness of their lives, the Dorsey band had reminded me that nothing much matters if you don't have the music, the swing. I'd looked into their faces, tired faces, faces behind which existed all kinds of individual pains, and watched them come alive when they were playing together. A bunch of guys who were one for a few hours every night, giving their all, giving their whole hearts. Take it or leave it. This is your life. Right here, right now.

That night in a dumpy motel, my face puffy and another solo road trip slated for tomorrow, I finally knew deep in my gut that there was only here, now. That there are no second chances. That all the questing, the pondering, the excuses were only an elaborate dodge-and-weave. Real life isn't lived in constant suspension. Only children believe that Christmas is a million years away. Only children wait for someone to say, "Can you come out to play?"

I climbed into bed, exhausted, but before turning off the light I scrawled on the backside of a road map I would use the next day: "Don't miss the off-ramp. It's where you live."

• • •

In the days and weeks following Hurricane Andrew, the eyes of residents in southern Florida remained perpetually glazed. The storm's violent suddenness brought a unique kind of hell, knocking the wind out of everyone without any real warning. Nothing was normal. Like travelers in a foreign land, people yearned for a bowl of cornflakes or the sports section. In a world where all the street signs, quite literally, were suddenly missing, they yearned for something—anything—familiar and easy. As with all such disasters, the whole story was impossible to tell. All the stock clichés were at hand: huge trees were split like kindling, trailers had been crushed like tin cans, towers had toppled like building blocks. There had been so much shock, and it had struck so hard and fast.

"At first people just said, 'I'm alive. I'm alive!'" said Meda Jensen, who managed a Florida City visitor's center that became a military command post after the storm. "This sounds really trivial, but as soon as they opened I just had to go get my nails done. It was just something normal that I could do."

It was amid all this wreckage and dislocation that I pulled off a state road onto a gravel road for no particular reason and there found William T. "W. T." Turner, contentedly smoking a generic-brand cigarette. "Yap," he said, "it's pretty bad. Pretty damned bad. No doubt about that."

But he'd already moved on. There was work to be done. "When you don't have anything to do, you start meditating on what you should or could have been," he warned, in his plain-spoken philosophical way.

With that, I entered W. T.'s world. And it should be

said up-front that in W. T.'s world, there is no "bull-skating." It was a term he used repeatedly and though I've never been able to find it any dictionary, I think I caught the drift. "You take a look at the world, it all boils down to choice," he said in an inimitable twang. "We make good choices. We make bad choices. But you can still always choose to do something good. Hell," he said, "I wouldn't view being an ex-felon as a hindrance. It may hurt, but it's not all she wrote."

He was true to his word. Something of a journeyman worker, he'd been called down from his home in northern Florida to put a roof on the local jail. He couldn't do it alone, and so he'd talked prison officials into letting him enlist some of the inmates. "Hell, they can learn a skill," he said. "They're all god-damned delinquents, if you want the truth. But four of six of 'em is like my sons. Just don't let 'em know they scare ya."

With that disclaimer W. T. and I headed in. The crew he soon introduced me to didn't seem too frightening at all. They understood that there would be "no bull-skating."

"Get over here. See this? It ain't right," he barked at one of his men. "It should be even here. And don't leave that piece hanging out. You see that? That's a sloppy job. We don't do sloppy work." He had a growl in his voice, but his charges didn't seem to mind. They also heard the soft spot within his barreled chest.

"In seven years of doing this, I've got letters that thank me for showing them a way to make an honest living. Hell, I've been doing this roofing thing for thirty-nine years," said W. T., who would only cop to being twenty-three years old. "Some come around and tell me, 'Well I got caught stealing or doping or this or that.' I remember one guy coming up to me with real shaky hands. They just shook all the time. But I give him a pencil and tape measure and he started to know the business. So I give 'em a little sermon on that. Soon they're calling me 'Boss.' And some of 'em when they leave, they hug me and, don't you know, they start crying. And I think it's because they felt like for the first time somebody cared."

Now don't get him wrong. W. T. wasn't the least bit interested in coddling these guys, even if he did provide the occasional barbecue. They were veterans of the streets and state prison system. They were in for pimping and drug trafficking, theft and assault. And not a few would do anything to wheedle their disingenuous way into whatever good graces might pave the easiest path out. But W. T. handpicked his crews very carefully, going solely on gut, choosing twelve men who didn't have too much attitude to take directions or too little commitment to work in 90-degree heat. It was a look in their eyes, he said. That's how he knew. And there was also a distinct smell, the smell of a man who still had some heart.

It was hotter than blazes up on the roof, tar soaking up an unforgiving midday sun. The men swung pickaxes and hatchets, smoothed the wind-torn areas for 4-by-8- foot sheets of insulation then to be laid over with 30 pounds per square foot of asphalt. It was hot. Real hot. The roof was high. And the convicted felons had in their hands some serious equipment.

"The boss is a good man. A real good man," said Jerry Duckworth, grinning like a cat with his mouth full of feathers. The crew's No. 1 sweet-talker was at work, quickly zeroing in. "Hey Boss, so you got a cigarette, Boss?"

W. T. laughed along. It was part of the patter, he said, but it only went so far. Everyone knew the line and when it was crossed, when it was time to get serious. "This is on-the-job training, the best you can get," said Anthony

Bush, a sweet-faced guy with two years left on a drug-trafficking conviction. "Now when I get out, there'll be something I can do. Otherwise, I'd go back to the dope. That's what I'd do."

That's exactly what a lot of young ex-convicts do. They get out of prison with little skill or experience or sense of connection to a better world and so all too often end up back behind bars. Blame it on whomever you like. It is reality, and it costs all of us. W. T., of course, would not admit to being part of any public service-type program. He was just doing a basic thing, and after all it was an exchange. These guys helped him, too.

When his crew was done, W. T. planned to bring them down to a nearby lake for some fishing and barbecue. Some of the guys would have less than a month left before moving out, now with some hope of earning more than minimum wage. "And I'll have told 'em what it is to screw up. Plain and simple. And they'll have listened or not. I'll have told 'em, 'You got to concentrate. Down on the ground you can sing, dance, pray, whatever you want. But up here on my roof, I'm the last word. You're gonna listen to me like young people once did their daddies.' And like I say, some will listen. Others won't. But, at least from what I seen, a lot of them listen."

W. T. recoiled a moment. "I sound like a damned preacher," he said. "But these kids have had no guidance. Maybe their daddies is in a bar or off the scene altogether. I don't know. But I see it all the time. And it makes me mad. . . . I ain't bragging on myself, but I'm giving them something to learn. Like a daddy would."

And like a daddy, when the job was done and his trainees had given him big, long hugs, "then I'll just about start crying. I hate that. But it's a damn good feeling." It was, he said, a feeling he couldn't quite define.

And, truly, who can? It is one part do-good spirit, one part the sense of fulfillment the do-gooder gets out of the deal. It was one part, for W. T. at least, "tough love." But it was also a dose tempered with the patient love of a father. Most of all it is one small door opening, a door through which maybe only a few will actually stride. But by W. T.'s sights, that would be a few that might do better in life than his alcoholic daddy once did.

"You see, I'm self-educated myself," W. T. said before we parted. "I had to quit school in the seventh grade to help my mother out. We were sharecroppers. We were six boys and two girls who picked cotton. I knew I could do something better. . . . And so when I meet these guys, they catch on. They know I'm not bull-skating. They know I want to make something go here. That's what we all want, right? The guys that work for me, they've got something to learn, something they think about at night. And the next day, I ease 'em into something new. And then they go one step further. There are shortcuts on cutting and insulation. But I watch 'em struggle for awhile, try to figure it out on their own. That's what all of us have got to do. Then, after a time, I'll say, 'Here, Shorty, this is how it's done.' And we work on the shortcut together. After a while, the work gets finished. And we both feel pretty damned good."

How badly we all want to feel good, to feel happy, to feel valued. How simple it is, for however complicated we've made it. Buy more books. Visit more health clubs. Divorce your spouse, move to a new town. Denounce politicians and the press. Hate people of a different color or sexual orientation. Blame people who subscribe to a religious code different from your own.

Go ahead.

But what will remain is this: It's all a lot of bull-skating.

William T. "W.T." Turner takes a break from work on the Dade Correctional Institution at Florida City, Florida.

We're artful at it. We're sophisticated. We package it as morality, consign it to politics or fate. We say we deserve something better, then wait for someone else to do the work. And what is that 'something better' after all? A lot of the time we simply lose sight, slowly and suddenly.

W. T. wasn't the most articulate or educated man. He'd be the first to say that he was rough around the edges. He carried personal prejudices and ugly, secret little scars. He wasn't a hero and readily admitted it. But that wasn't much the point, either. Life is about rough edges and regeneration, about living with old wounds and finding new ways to heal. Life is mainly just short, and you can stop there.

Or you can test your reach, stretch out a bit farther.

There is a lot to see and hear and do. When it comes to building a home, making a solid life, "there ain't no room for bull-skating," as W. T. might say.

The time for bull-skating has passed.

• • •

When people have asked over the months what this book is about, I've mostly said I don't quite know. It hasn't the weight of a scholarly study or history's well-documented heft. It offers no linear narrative or sturdy prescription. It's only a quilt, a mishmash of stories filled with all kinds of flaws. In a way, though, the flaws are at the heart of it all. We are a nation still growing, still testing our wobbly wings. We are still searching for a happy medium, that solid place where our sights aren't set too low and our expectations aren't too high. The best I can hope is that it offers some hope and poses a modest challenge.

Whatever you're doing, stop doing nothing. Wherever you are, don't look away.

I know it's likely that much of what I've covered in these pages has seemed off-target—not quite what you perceive, not quite what's familiar, not quite something that applies. It's the Cosmo quiz effect: The questions and answers never entirely fit. But that isn't really the point.

There are people far better equipped than I to help link neighbor with neighbor, point the way to programs that work and citizens who care. But first we must begin talking and truly hearing one another. This book is ultimately only a small stab at opening a dialogue that might help us refind our voices and hearts. The larger challenge is to go still farther, beyond conversation, into the realm of action. We all have every right to tune in angry radio hosts, laugh at politicians, loathe bureaucrats, lambaste people whose circumstances we don't understand. All of us have every right to drop a few coins in the Muscular Dystrophy display at the mall, vote the party line every four years and consider that more than enough.

But it's not. Not if you're bull-skating.

True grown-ups go the extra mile, see where they are and make a serious stab at creating something true, something real. The rights that we cherish come with solemn obligations. Whatever we think, whoever we blame, the work we have to do in life remains the same. And curses to whoever started the rumor that it would be easy.

I've got a friend named John Galvin. To some in his hometown he's known as "the trash man." To me he is Don Quixote, a guy seized by ideas and passion and a desire truly to be in this world before he dies. Early one morning a while back he called to check in, catching me before I'd fully awakened. Because he's him and I'm me, we were deep into a rumination on life before my first cup of coffee. What is a soul mate? Why are we here? What does it take to be a "good" person? I imagined John, a postal worker, a father nearing fifty, down in Kentucky, pacing back and forth smoking cigarettes in the family room. Talking to me, a single woman scrunched up in a rocking chair deep in New York City, an ambulance's siren blaring nearby. An odd couple, dopily trying to figure out life.

I love John Galvin because he cares enough to act. He's depressed sometimes, unsure about the course of his life, troubled by the empty places, urgent about his need to fill them up. But this does not stop him. He, like so many remarkable people I've met, chooses to dive in. The urge to live a meaningful, dignified life fills his heart.

"This has been the loneliest, the hardest, the most expensive thing I could ever do. But it's an existential thing," he told me when we met at his home in Kentucky a few years back. "Do you put your feet on the floor every morning just to work, to eat, to support and raise your family?" he asked, his eyes burning straight into mine.

"Of course, it's all those things," he said. "But, my gosh, it's also got to be about something more."

I'd driven up a broad street lined with shrubs shifting lazily in the afternoon breeze to find John Galvin out behind his house, considering the prospects for a shade garden he'd planted under the arms of a particularly shady tree. His wife was polite but quickly excused herself. I was one more intruder, a reporter after a story, one more dubious by-product of her husband's obsessive campaign. Soon we were seated together on a sofa in his family's living room, but Galvin kept springing up, tugging on cigarettes, quoting favorite authors at random. I wondered if he wasn't a little half-cocked. Yet something in him was indelibly sane.

Galvin was on a crusade, afraid that some years from now, when the plastic linings of the new waste dumps that had cropped up all around Kentucky were full, the bill would come due. He feared that this refuse, which had been trucked in from miles away, would end up exacting an unconscionably high price. Like many people drawn into social activism of all sorts, Galvin had been a reluctant participant. At first his only interest was in the fishing at Clear Creek, a special place where he and his son had idled away happy afternoons. Quickly, though, he'd been drawn into battle with a $30 billion dollar landfill business that was not managed by amateurs. When they planned a dump near his beloved creek, Galvin was drawn into a fierce fight.

By the time we met, that particular skirmish was at a stand-off. Clear Creek was fine for now, Galvin said, but the things he'd learned in the struggle had made him just angry enough to press on, and on. Beyond anything he'd planned for or anything his family could quite understand. "I've seen it in a very moralistic sense. This is something that I can do something about. It's a passion. I probably wore people out on the topic several years ago," he said. "But I can't help it. I don't want these guys to have anyplace to hide."

By "these guys," he meant unsavory characters who had cashed in on the 1980s trend toward privatization, reshaping the rules for interstate trash-dumping. Some in the industry, which has been associated with Mafia types, were approaching rural towns where citizens weren't well organized, where land values were depressed and local zoning boards uneducated and weak. They were proposing what seemed like a pretty good deal: Sell us your land and we'll keep local dumping fees low. In exchange, out-of-state refuse would be trucked in—for a price.

"Don't worry about this bunch," a garbage entrepreneur on his way to a local zoning board meeting was heard to say. "They're just ignorant rednecks."

This made John Galvin mad. In decades past, outside interests had stripped Kentucky's coal fields and slashed their forests to provide wood for buildings out East. Now, it seemed to him, his state was facing a new wave of exploitation. As he recounted this scenario, a certain fever rose in the postal worker's voice. He quoted Faulkner and Melville and Dostoyevsky and Twain. He pulled dog-eared files from among mountains heaped by his dining room table. Over time he'd accumulated a whole library of information that even federal agents had come to rely on. "I stopped counting what it cost $20,000 ago. Hours on the phone, the bills sometimes $400 and more," he said, displaying a neat, if tired notebook ledger. "We've given up family vacations and new things. There have been some real battles fought in this den. There has been a lot of pain."

And still, he had kept on. John Galvin, your fairly average guy, had taken what started out as a small, personal stand and seen it through to something much bigger. From his family's brick house, he'd formed alliances with law enforcement officials and environmentalists and journalists nationwide.

"I don't know what drives John. It's an enigma, really," said Jim Malone, a Kentucky reporter who had also worked tirelessly to uncover the individual stories behind the anonymous businessmen trucking in trash. "John has been able to put a lot of things together that other people miss. He has an eye for addresses and names. He's been able to make the links. All kinds of people have called on him for help. And it was always for free. He's nearly spent himself under pursuing this."

What drives John Galvin is something more than self-interest, something far harder to pin down. Even he couldn't say exactly what has pushed him so far. Once he got in, it just somehow seemed impossible to get out. He said his proudest effort had perhaps been in helping to shut down a site at Roe Creek in nearby Lawrence County. The word was that out-of-state haulers were bringing in asbestos and depositing it at an unsafe landfill. And so his by-now familiar research began.

Galvin, a mustachioed man whose eyes are intensely blue, started with a roster of the companies involved, writing a contact at the New York Department of Environmental Conservation. Fourteen violations could immediately be linked to the list. He got a copy of a solid waste regulation report from New Jersey and quickly matched hundreds more violations. He spoke with a state investigator in New Jersey, tracked down a racketeering complaint in Long Island, New York. Still more connections, still more questions and concerns. Some entities had cagily changed their names, but Galvin traced them to the same addresses. Some were based in one place, operating from another. But through the help of his homegrown network, he pinned down criminal records, private histories, all kinds of information that helped to turn the tide.

Many others contributed: activists in Lawrence County and Jim Malone, the local reporter who dug some more and synthesized the information in stories that heightened the pressure. Officials listened and before long closed down the Roe Creek site. Legislation eventually followed, requiring background checks of all potential landfill operators in Kentucky.

A few years ago, when all this began, Galvin had known none of these people. He had no connections, no money, no clout. He was up against some fairly formidable players, but he had refused to take a dive. "The bad guys have been arrogant. They are sleazebags who have been able to move around the country undetected because there's no central pool of information. No one has been dogging them," said Galvin.

It wasn't all that difficult. It had just taken tenacity and a commitment larger than he could really afford. Chris Manthey, a thirty-year-old corporate researcher in New York, met Galvin several years ago through Brian Lipsett, who was working with an environmental group founded by Lois Gibbs after "Love Canal."

"There's this guy from Kentucky who keeps bothering me and bothering me and won't stop," Lipsett told Manthey, who wanted to volunteer.

"And it's true," said Manthey, who since has devoted scores of hours to background investigations. "At times my commitment has wavered, but his has not. He has this big picture in mind."

All three men eventually came to work as a team. Galvin continued to make phone calls, round up commission reports, dig up court records. Lipsett worked with citizen groups and individuals looking for help. Manthey donated what time he could to searching through databases, adding yet more information to their growing bank.

"This is the hard way," said Galvin. "There are smart ways. You've got all these people fighting all these separate battles. But no one is winning the war."

They'd come up with an alternative: a national database that would centralize all Galvin's work and the work of many others. Anyone in anyplace around the country would be able to tap in and learn in seconds for a modest price the backgrounds of proposed land-buyers in their area. "People would have a silver bullet and, when necessary, could stop the bad guys without going through what my family has," said Galvin.

Together, Lipsett and Galvin and Manthey incorporated EBIC, the nonprofit Environmental Background Information Center. With only about $200 in the bank, they planned to write grant applications, planned to network, planned to start forming the database of their dreams. But Manthey had also recently married, started his own consulting firm and bought his first home. Lipsett was in Pennsylvania, finishing up a graduate degree in criminology. And, Galvin said, "I've done almost all I can do. I've pushed the limit of my family's emotional and financial budget."

Some months after my article was published, I called to check in. Galvin reported receiving hundreds of phone calls and as many donations, mostly made in the form of small personal checks. "When you think of it, it's really pretty amazing. These people who read a story in the newspaper over Sunday breakfast were actually touched enough to track us down," Galvin said. Some months after that, he was invited to the White House, where he was honored for his American heroism.

I've seen so many people make the extra steps that John Galvin has. Don't believe it when someone tells you that people don't care. In these pages alone is proof that something far finer is there.

John Galvin was tired, but remained committed to his particular cause. He'd discovered that you *can* fight city hall, that the "little guy" *can* in fact win. Not all of the time. But just often enough to make it worth meeting the challenge. When things got to be overwhelming for Galvin, whenever the pall of discouragement set in, he reminded himself of an uncredited quotation he'd clipped from a grassroots environmental newsletter: "Nothing in the world can take the place of persistence. Talent will not; nothing is more common than unsuccessful men with talent. Genius will not; unrewarded genius is almost a proverb. Education will not; the world is full of educational derelicts. Persistence and determination alone are omnipotent."

Galvin said he would not always fight this passionately. Crusading was never part of his life plan. As he paced back and forth in the family room the Sunday afternoon I visited, he seemed a bit trapped, almost like a shackled animal exhausted by repeated efforts to break free. Others, he said, were sure to see the trucks coming into their own hometowns in years to come. Others, he hoped, would someday join in his fight.

"And see, then," said Galvin, "then maybe I could just go fishing again."

At the time I believed him. Now I think differently. He can't fully check out. He cares too much about being alive. He's got such a short time on this planet. No shorter a time than any of us, but for this man the opportunity called life is something vivid and urgent and real. He's a kid, full of naiveté and fueled by a broad, open heart. He's also hungry and stupid and willful. Like Don Quixote, he is doomed to failure and pain.

He doesn't care. Ultimately, he's the grown-up we all might be, if we weren't so afraid.

• • •

I have a big yellow-striped barn cat whose name is Bruno Ray. Together we have made several moves now. As I write this, our life is halfpacked in a bunch of numbered boxes. We are preparing to move, relocate once again. I'm always glad to have him with me, glad he lives at my next new address. Sometimes late at night, when other tenants in my building are undoubtedly sleeping, Bruno and I curl up on the floor and listen to a symphony together from start to finish. Other times, when I'm furiously typing away at my desk, he jumps up to sit beside my printer and telephone, keeping a long, quiet vigil until the last sentence is written and we can both go and rest. This likable cat likes to grumble at birds, belching frustrated yowls while crouched at the window. He can't stalk or catch these birds, for they fly too high off the ground. We live where we live. The birds are able to glide far beyond.

Oh, how he wants to fly, though. It's the Indiana, the restless cat in him.

In truth, Bruno and I fell together reluctantly. He would have been happy to stay where he was, out on a farm deep in the country. And for my part, I thought a cat would only tie down the footloose reporter, crimp my free-wheeling style. But when Donna Ray called from Indiana, there was nothing else to do. "We have a kitten we want you to have," she said, and a few days later I was on a plane. The Bruno-monster, whether he liked it or not, was transported into my world, and there was nothing he could do about it, nothing he could do to stave off the change.

He was a symbol, I guess, for both the Ray family and me. We had been brought together by the ugliest of circumstances. A tornado had ripped through the family's trailer, exploding its four flimsy walls. Debris spread for miles around. Amidst the wreckage lay Benjamin, the lifeless body of their cherished infant son. He had been sucked from his mother's arms as she ran for cover. Though they survived, Tim and Donna Ray, as well as their elder daughters, had been spewed out like ragdolls, along with all their worldly possessions. The family was battered, in shock, when I showed up. My professional demeanor left me only that much more appalled. As we sat in a hotel room just after the storm had hit, wiping away so much of their lives, I could not absorb all the sadness. I sat like a half-numb lump, off to the side, dispassionately recording their pain. Why these people let me in I'll never know. A reporter had no business intruding on their bewilderment and loss. It felt like a ghoulish lowpoint in my career. But somehow, because these were such giving people, they did not begrudge me my job. They felt safe enough, they said, to talk. In our talking, they said, there was something healing and fine.

When it was all done, my tear-jerking story filed, we all shook hands and I was on my way. But something had happened, that magical thing I often find out on the road. A bond had been made, something that endured, stayed. The Rays kept in touch well after the storm. Friendship was unexpected, more than I deserved to find. When the time came many months later, they wanted me to have one of their newborn kittens. Bruno was our witness, proof that from the most dormant ashes new life can and does eventually spring.

I give Bruno food every day and a bed to lie on. Not a lot more. But we've got a compact. I do this little bit and he is there for me, all the time. So the date was a bore. So the story is only half written. So my apartment feels small and my ideal town is about a million miles away. So I'm half drunk or half cocked or occasionally bleary. There's Bruno, the picture of Zen. Whatever I do, regardless of my failings, he needs me. And I'll be damned if I don't rely a little on him.

He is a daily reminder of the lie in creeping detachment. The Rays were crying, lost in their pain. And there I was, taking notes, a firm grip on myself. Their tears weren't my tears. This was the lie I told myself, a lie that made me feel clammy and old. There is no dignity in ducking. There isn't even any truth in it. If you think you live alone, take another look. There are all these other people around you, slipping through while you examine the hole in your heart.

For years I've had a major problem with flowers. Send me a bouquet and I almost immediately feel sad. From the moment the glorious arrangement arrives, it is already dying. I trim the stems daily, carefully, and assiduously change the water. But it does no good. Each morning the petals are a little more wilted, curling, dropping constantly to the floor. I try to hang on, but like the monkey clutching the nut from inside his cage, it's a self-defeating game.

Let it go. I tell myself this. But it is so hard to begin again.

How many times will I have to learn that the things we least want are often the very things we most need? I've run far and fast in search of some peace, now only to find it's been everywhere, around me all the time. It is in the people I've met in all kinds of unlikely places. It's in the openness and fundamental good-heartedness I've met time and again on the road. It's in the hopes held by the kids who show up on Saturdays to study at The Dome and in the bravery of Miss Rose, who prays each morning at dawn. It is in all the many Americans who have extended a hand: poets in truck stops and preachers, teachers and politicians and parents. How dumb I was not to hear their voices, see their faces, even as they were swelling, growing stronger, gathering all around. They were so closeby.

In my adolescence I slammed my bedroom door, eager to retreat from the noisy world outside. Well into adulthood I stayed two steps back, a respectable child of fortune. But I'd missed the simplest lesson of all: Happiness is made by the people who care, the blessings they share, the heart they refuse to hide, even knowing it may break.

This is something children must learn, and adults ought to know.

You do not have to choose all the time. Sometimes you've only the gray space. Reading *People* magazine doesn't mean you can't read thoughtful literature. Dropping out for a weekend of solitude doesn't mean you can't join in, be active, go forward with a ringing vote another day. It is not always east or west, left or right. It is often the turbulent middle ground, the part most difficult to hold, that carries the seeds of our dearest goals. We are all the time rushing, usually to this or that extreme, counting the wrongs, distracted by what we think we deserve. It is not easy to embrace the clutter and still join in. But, alas, that's where life is: Down deep in the mess, rooted in our willingness to dig in. It is not technology or politics, money, adventure or physical beauty that sustain. It is people's hopes. People's dreams. Our ability, each of us, to grow and change. Every day.

Without realizing it, I've sped past home countless times. But because I didn't know this it was never quite there. I was too busy looking ahead and behind, forever making choices in a world where nothing is sure. We all suffer myopia, at least from time to time, our eyes alternately fixed on the road or overwhelmed by the broad horizons. I've found scanty conclusions and no epitaph in the miles I've traveled. But looking around at my pile of boxes, a broom and dustpan in the corner, the mismatched mementos and one yellow cat, I see the fragments of a life soon to be moved on to that next somewhere I'll never own. I see a journey constantly ending, and beginning again. This is the rhythm. This is the swing.

There are all these faces, voices, snatches passed in confusion and defeat. In them lie all the answers we're ever likely to get. In the cramped, chaotic, imperfect little boxes we constantly build and then smash, there is the true sense of home. These are the things that we carry. There is life in these things.

So what if they aren't what was promised? So what if you're disappointed or scared?

Growing up is about building a home, getting a life, making something of what's already there.